# COOK'S KITCHEN

# Quick and Easy

igloobooks

# igloobooks

*Published in 2017*
*by Igloo Books Ltd*
*Cottage Farm*
*Sywell*
*NN6 0BJ*
*www.igloobooks.com*

*Food photography and recipe development © Stockfood, the Food Media Agency*
*Cover images © Stockfood, the Food Media Agency*

*STA002 0617*
*4 6 8 10 9 7 5 3*
*ISBN: 978-1-78440-825-1*

*Printed and manufactured in China*

# Contents

# Breakfasts and Brunches

# Waffles with Bacon and Maple Syrup

---

**SERVES 4**

**PREPARATION TIME 10 MINUTES**

**COOKING TIME 20 MINUTES**

---

## INGREDIENTS

1 tbsp vegetable oil, for greasing

275 g / 10 oz / 1 ¾ cups plain (all-purpose) flour, sifted

150 g / 5 oz / ⅔ cup caster (superfine) sugar

2 tsp baking powder

a pinch of salt

2 medium eggs, separated

250 ml / 9 fl. oz / 1 cup whole milk

175 g / 6 oz / ¾ cup unsalted butter, melted

1 tsp vanilla extract

8 rashers of streaky bacon

150 ml / 5 fl. oz / ⅔ cup maple syrup, to serve

a small handful of raspberries, to garnish

## METHOD

- Preheat a waffle iron according to the manufacturer's instructions. Grease with vegetable oil.

- Combine the flour, sugar, baking powder and salt in a large mixing bowl and stir briefly.

- In a separate bowl, beat the egg yolks and then beat in the milk, butter and vanilla extract.

- Beat the egg whites in another bowl until stiffly peaked and fold into the batter.

- Spoon into the preheated waffle iron and cook the waffles in batches, according to the manufacturer's instructions, until golden brown.

- Remove from the iron and leave to cool slightly. Preheat the grill to hot.

- Cook the bacon for 2 minutes on each side until golden and crisp. Drain on kitchen paper.

- Stack the waffles, drizzle with syrup and serve with the bacon and a garnish of raspberries.

**TOP TIP**

Let the waffles cool on a wire rack to maintain their crispness.

# Breakfast Bruschettas

## SERVES 4

## PREPARATION TIME 20 MINUTES

## INGREDIENTS

½ red onion, finely chopped
450 g / 1 lb / 3 cups vine tomatoes, cored
   and diced
¼ tsp caster (superfine) sugar
1 clove of garlic, minced
75 ml / 3 fl. oz / ⅓ cup olive oil
a small bunch of flat-leaf parsley, chopped
1 white baguette, sliced and toasted
salt and freshly ground black pepper

## METHOD

- Combine the onion, tomatoes, sugar, garlic, olive oil, parsley and seasoning in a mixing bowl.

- Stir well, cover and leave to stand for 10 minutes.

- Spoon onto slices of the baguette and serve.

**TOP TIP**
Try using chopped basil instead of parsley.

# French Toast with Banana

## METHOD

- Whisk together the milk, eggs and cinnamon in a large shallow bowl or dish.
- Dip the slices of bread into the bowl to coat both sides.
- Heat a knob of butter in a large frying pan set over a medium heat until hot. Fry the soaked bread for 1–2 minutes each side until golden brown.
- Repeat for each serving, using fresh butter for each batch.
- Stack and serve with sliced banana, walnuts and maple syrup on top.

**SERVES 4**

**PREPARATION TIME 5 MINUTES**

**COOKING TIME 20 MINUTES**

## INGREDIENTS

150 ml / 5 fl. oz / ⅔ cup semi-skimmed milk
4 medium eggs
a pinch of ground cinnamon
8 slices of white bread
55 g / 2 oz / ¼ cup unsalted butter, cubed
2 small bananas, sliced
75 g / 3 oz / ¾ cup walnuts, chopped
110 ml / 4 fl. oz / ½ cup maple syrup

**TOP TIP**
Try a dollop of raspberry or strawberry jam (jelly) on top instead of maple syrup or banana.

# Pancakes with Blueberries

**SERVES 4**

**PREPARATION TIME 10 MINUTES**

**COOKING TIME 15 MINUTES**

## INGREDIENTS

250 ml / 9 fl. oz / 1 cup whole milk

2 small eggs

2 tbsp butter, melted and cooled

75 g / 3 oz / ½ cup plain (all-purpose)
    flour, sifted

55 g / 2 oz / ⅓ cup buckwheat flour, sifted

1 tbsp caster (superfine) sugar

2–3 tbsp sunflower oil

225 g / 8 oz / 2 cups blueberries

110 g / 4 oz / ½ cup light agave nectar

## METHOD

- Whisk together the milk, eggs and butter in a large mixing bowl. Add both flours and the sugar and gradually whisk until you have a smooth batter.

- Remove the pancake batter and heat a teaspoon of the sunflower oil in a frying pan set over a medium heat until hot.

- Add small ladles of the batter and dot them with blueberries. Cook until golden and set underneath before flipping them. Cook for a further minute or so until golden.

- Remove to a warm plate and cover loosely with aluminium foil. Cook the remaining batter in the same way, using fresh oil for each batch.

- Serve the cooked pancakes with agave nectar and any remaining blueberries on top.

**TOP TIP**

Try these pancakes with chopped strawberries instead of blueberries.

# Fruity Granola with Yoghurt

**SERVES 4**

**PREPARATION TIME 10 MINUTES**

**COOKING TIME 2 MINUTES**

## INGREDIENTS

225 g / 8 oz / 1 ½ cups rolled oats
75 g / 3 oz / ½ cup raisins
75 g / 3 oz / ¾ cup almonds
2 tbsp dried papaya
2 tbsp dried pineapple
2 tbsp sunflower oil
a pinch of ground cinnamon
600 g / 1 lb 5 oz / 3 cups Greek yoghurt
125 g / 4 ½ oz / 1 cup blueberries
150 g / 5 oz / 1 cup strawberries, hulled
  and chopped
1 passion fruit, halved
1 mango, pitted and scored
350 ml / 12 fl. oz / 1 ½ cups semi-skimmed
  milk, to serve

## METHOD

- Toss together the oats, raisins, almonds, papaya, pineapple, oil and cinnamon in a mixing bowl.

- Preheat the grill to a moderate heat. Spread the granola mixture out on a large tray. Toast for 2 minutes, stirring after 1 minute.

- Spoon the yoghurt into bowls and top with the toasted granola. Serve with the fresh fruit on top and the milk on the side.

**TOP TIP**
Try adding a handful of sunflower seeds to the granola for an extra crunch.

# Apple Muffins

**MAKES 12**

**PREPARATION TIME 10 MINUTES**

**COOKING TIME 25 MINUTES**

## INGREDIENTS

300 g / 10 ½ oz / 2 cups self-raising
    flour, sifted
½ tsp baking powder
½ tsp bicarbonate of (baking) soda
a pinch of salt
110 g / 4 oz / ½ cup margarine, softened
175 g / 6 oz / ¾ cup caster (superfine) sugar
75 g / 3 oz / ⅓ cup apple purée
2 large eggs
1 tsp vanilla extract
1 large Braeburn apple, cored and sliced

## METHOD

- Preheat the oven to 190°C (170°C fan) / 375F / gas 5 and line a 12-hole muffin tin with muffin cases.

- Combine the flour, baking powder, bicarbonate of soda and salt in a large mixing bowl.

- Beat together the margarine, sugar, apple purée, eggs and vanilla extract in a separate mixing bowl until smooth.

- Fold in the flour mixture until just combined. Spoon into the muffin cases and top with a slice of apple.

- Bake for 22–25 minutes until golden, risen and springy to the touch.

- Remove to a wire rack to cool before serving.

**TOP TIP**
Add ½ tsp of ground cinnamon to the batter for some warming spice.

# Breakfast Bars

**SERVES 8**

**PREPARATION TIME 5 MINUTES**

**COOKING TIME 20 MINUTES**

## INGREDIENTS

300 g / 10 ½ oz / 2 cups rolled oats
100 g / 3 ½ oz / ⅔ cup raisins
4 tbsp flaxseeds
110 g / 4 oz / ½ cup apple sauce
75 ml / 3 fl. oz / ⅓ cup sunflower oil
a pinch of salt

## METHOD

- Preheat the oven to 180°C (160°C fan) / 350F / gas 4 and line an 18 cm (7 in) square baking tin with greaseproof paper.

- Combine the oats, raisins and flaxseeds in a large mixing bowl.

- Melt together the apple sauce, sunflower oil and salt in a saucepan set over a medium heat.

- Whisk until smooth before pouring over the oats. Stir well to combine before packing the mixture into the prepared tin.

- Bake for 15–20 minutes until golden on top. Remove the tin to a wire rack to cool completely before turning out and cutting into bars.

**TOP TIP**
For a touch of luxury, add a handful of chocolate chips to the ingredients.

# Omelette with Salmon

**MAKES 4**

**PREPARATION TIME 10 MINUTES**

**COOKING TIME 20 MINUTES**

## INGREDIENTS

12 medium eggs
55 g / 2 oz / ¼ cup unsalted butter, cubed
225 g / 8 oz / 1 ½ cups smoked salmon, sliced
½ lemon, juiced
a small handful of rocket (arugula)
a small handful of watercress
a small bunch of chives
100 g / 3 ½ oz / ½ cup plain yoghurt
salt and freshly ground black pepper

## METHOD

- Preheat the grill to hot.
- For each omelette, beat three of the eggs in a bowl with plenty of salt and pepper.
- Melt a knob or two of butter in an omelette or frying pan set over a moderate heat until hot.
- Add the beaten egg and tilt the pan to coat the surface, letting the egg set underneath. Pull the set egg towards the centre to let the uncooked egg slide underneath.
- Move the omelette to the grill to brown on top for 1 minute. Top with the smoked salmon, rocket, watercress, chives, yoghurt and seasoning.
- Repeat steps 2 through 5 for each omelette.

**TOP TIP**

Beat the eggs thoroughly, making sure they are frothy, then pour into the pan.

# Chopped Fruit Salad

## SERVES 4

## PREPARATION TIME 15 MINUTES

## INGREDIENTS

1 mango, pitted, peeled and diced
½ pineapple, peeled, cored and diced
150 g / 5 oz / 1 cup strawberries, hulled
    and halved
125 g / 4 ½ oz / 1 cup raspberries
125 g / 4 ½ oz / 1 cup blueberries
125 g / 4 ½ oz / 1 cup blackberries
250 ml / 9 fl. oz / 1 cup orange juice
a few sprigs of mint, to garnish

## METHOD

- Toss together the fruit with the orange juice in a mixing bowl.
- Spoon into bowls and serve with a garnish of mint.

**TOP TIP**
Serve this fruit salad with a dollop of vanilla or plain yoghurt on top.

# Cheese Toastie

**MAKES 4**

**PREPARATION TIME 5 MINUTES**

**COOKING TIME 10 MINUTES**

## INGREDIENTS

8 slices of white bread
55 g / 2 oz / ¼ cup butter, softened
300 g / 10 ½ oz / 3 cups Cheddar, sliced
2 tbsp tarragon, chopped

## METHOD

- Preheat the oven to 180°C (160°C fan) / 350F / gas 4.
- Butter the slices of bread and sit half, butter side-down, on a baking tray.
- Top with the cheese and then place the other slice of bread, butter side-up, on top.
- Bake for 6–7 minutes, flipping after 3–4 minutes, until golden.
- Remove the toasties, cut in half and garnish with chopped parsley before serving.

**TOP TIP**
Try a combination of cheeses such as mozzarella and Taleggio.

# Herby Eggs on Toast

## METHOD

- Preheat the grill to hot. Toast the slices of bread until golden on both sides.

- Heat a large saucepan of water over a moderate heat until simmering. Stir in the white wine vinegar.

- Crack the eggs into cups and slide into the water, poaching for 3 minutes.

- Meanwhile, top the slices of toast with grated cheese, then grill for 1–2 minutes until the cheese is melted and bubbling.

- Remove the poached eggs with a slotted spoon. Drain on kitchen paper.

- Cut the slices of toast in half and place on plates. Top with the poached eggs and garnish with a little salt, pepper and chopped parsley before serving.

## SERVES 4

## PREPARATION TIME 10 MINUTES

## COOKING TIME 10 MINUTES

## INGREDIENTS

4 thick slices of white bread
1 tbsp white wine vinegar
150 g / 5 oz / 1 ½ cups Cheddar, grated
4 large eggs
a small handful of flat-leaf parsley,
    finely chopped
salt and freshly ground black pepper

**TOP TIP**
Try a couple of dashes of Worcestershire sauce on the toast for a spicy addition.

# Smoked Salmon Bagels

**MAKES 4**

**PREPARATION TIME 10 MINUTES**

**COOKING TIME 5 MINUTES**

## INGREDIENTS

4 bagels, split
150 g / 5 oz / 1 cup smoked salmon, sliced
½ lemon, juiced
225 g / 8 oz / 1 cup cream cheese with chives
55 g / 2 oz / 1 cup watercress
55 g / 2 oz / 1 cup rocket (arugula)
salt and freshly ground black pepper

## METHOD

- Toast the bagels under a hot grill or in a toaster.
- Dress the salmon with lemon juice and season with a little pepper.
- Spread the bottom half of the toasted bagels with cream cheese. Top with the smoked salmon, watercress and rocket.
- Sit the tops of the bagels in place and cut in half before serving.

**TOP TIP**
Some thinly sliced red onion adds a little crunch and texture to these bagels.

31

# Fruit Smoothie

## METHOD

- Combine the milk, yoghurt, fruit and honey in a food processor or blender.
- Blend on high until smooth. Add the crushed ice, stir and blend for a further minute.
- Pour into glasses and serve.

## SERVES 4

## PREPARATION TIME 10 MINUTES

## INGREDIENTS

750 ml / 1 pint 6 fl. oz / 3 cups semi-skimmed milk
150 g / 5 oz / ⅔ cup plain yoghurt
150 g / 5 oz / 1 cup strawberries, hulled and chopped
125 g / 4 ½ oz / 1 cup blueberries
1 large banana, chopped
2 tbsp honey
110 g / 4 oz / ½ cup crushed ice

**TOP TIP**
Go dairy-free and replace the milk and yoghurt for almond versions.

# Speedy Soups
and Salads

# Pea Soup

## METHOD

- Heat the oil in a large saucepan set over a medium heat until hot. Add the onion and a little salt, sweating for 4 minutes until soft.
- Add all of the peas, saving a small handful, then cover with the stock and milk. Stir well until simmering.
- Cook for 10 minutes and then blend with a stick blender until smooth. Season to taste with salt and pepper.
- Ladle into bowls and serve with the reserved peas and a swirl of yoghurt.

## SERVES 4

## PREPARATION TIME 5 MINUTES

## COOKING TIME 20 MINUTES

## INGREDIENTS

2 tbsp sunflower oil
1 small onion, finely chopped
450 g / 1 lb / 3 cups fresh garden peas
750 ml / 1 pint 6 fl. oz / 3 cups vegetable stock
250 ml / 9 fl. oz / 1 cup semi-skimmed milk
110 g / 4 oz / ½ cup plain yoghurt
salt and freshly ground black pepper

**TOP TIP**

A little chopped gammon makes a perfect garnish for this soup.

# Butternut Squash and Almond Soup

**SERVES 4**

**PREPARATION TIME 5 MINUTES**

**COOKING TIME 20 MINUTES**

## INGREDIENTS

2 tbsp olive oil
1 clove of garlic, minced
1 small onion, finely chopped
500 g / 1 lb 2 oz / 2 ½ cups butternut squash, diced
750 ml / 1 pint 6 fl. oz / 3 cups vegetable stock
55 g / 2 oz / ½ cup flaked (slivered) almonds
salt and freshly ground black pepper

## METHOD

- Heat the olive oil in a large saucepan set over a medium heat until hot.

- Add the garlic, onion and a little salt, then sweat for 5 minutes until softened.

- Stir in the butternut squash and cover with the stock. Cook until simmering and then cook steadily for a further 10 minutes.

- Blend until smooth with a stick blender. Season to taste with salt and pepper.

- Ladle into bowls and serve with a sprinkling of flaked almonds and a little more pepper.

**TOP TIP**
A little Cayenne pepper adds a touch of spice to this soup.

# Sweetcorn Chowder

## METHOD

- Heat together the oil and butter in a large saucepan set over a moderate heat until hot.
- Add the onion, ham, carrot and potato, frying for 5 minutes until the vegetables are softened.
- Stir in the sweetcorn, stock and half of the parsley. Simmer, then cook for a further 10 minutes until the potato and carrots are tender.
- Season to taste and ladle into bowls, garnishing with the remaining parsley.

## SERVES 4

## PREPARATION TIME 10 MINUTES

## COOKING TIME 20 MINUTES

## INGREDIENTS

1 tbsp sunflower oil
1 tbsp butter
1 onion, finely chopped
150 g / 5 oz / 1 cup cooked ham, diced
2 carrots, peeled and diced
450 g / 1 lb / 3 cups white potatoes, peeled and diced
400 g / 14 oz / 2 cups canned sweetcorn, drained
1 l / 1 pint 16 fl. oz / 4 cups vegetable stock, hot
a small bunch of flat-leaf parsley, chopped
salt and freshly ground black pepper

## TOP TIP

Stir in a generous drizzle of cream just before serving for a creamy chowder.

# Tomato Soup

**SERVES 4**

**PREPARATION TIME 10 MINUTES**

**COOKING TIME 20 MINUTES**

## INGREDIENTS

2 tbsp olive oil

2 cloves of garlic, minced

400 g / 14 oz / 2 cups canned
    chopped tomatoes

250 ml / 9 fl. oz / 1 cup passata

750 ml / 1 pint 6 fl. oz / 3 cups vegetable
    stock, hot

55 g / 2 oz / 1 cup fresh breadcrumbs

2 tbsp extra-virgin olive oil

a small bunch of flat-leaf parsley, chopped

a pinch of paprika

salt and freshly ground black pepper

## METHOD

- Heat the olive oil in a large saucepan set over a medium heat until hot.

- Add the garlic and fry for 45 seconds, stirring throughout, until lightly golden. Stir in the chopped tomatoes, passata and stock.

- Cook until simmering, then continue to cook for a further 10 minutes. Stir in the breadcrumbs and blend with a stick blender until smooth.

- Season to taste. Ladle into bowls and garnish with a drizzle of extra-virgin olive oil, some chopped parsley and a pinch of paprika.

**TOP TIP**

Try 50 g / 2 oz / ½ cup of grated Parmesan in place of the breadcrumbs.

# Bean and Chickpea Soup

## SERVES 4

## PREPARATION TIME 5 MINUTES

## COOKING TIME 25 MINUTES

## INGREDIENTS

2 tbsp olive oil

1 onion, finely chopped

2 cloves of garlic, minced

400 g / 14 oz / 2 cups canned chickpeas
(garbanzo beans), drained

400 g / 14 oz / 2 cups canned cannellini
beans, drained

400 ml / 14 fl. oz / 1 ⅔ cups passata

750 ml / 1 pint 6 fl. oz / 3 cups vegetable
stock, hot

a small handful of flat-leaf parsley,
finely chopped

2 tbsp extra-virgin olive oil

8 thin toasts, to serve

salt and freshly ground black pepper

## METHOD

- Heat the oil in a large saucepan set
  over a medium heat until hot.

- Add the onion, garlic and a little salt,
  sweating for 5 minutes until soft.

- Add the beans, passata and stock.
  Stir well and cook until simmering.

- Simmer for 15 minutes until the
  beans are tender. Season to taste
  with salt and pepper.

- Spoon into bowls and garnish
  with chopped parsley, a drizzle of
  extra-virgin olive oil and serve
  with some toasts.

**TOP TIP**

Blitz the toasts in a food processor and spoon the breadcrumbs over the soup.

# Chicken Soup

**SERVES 4**

**PREPARATION TIME 10 MINUTES**

**COOKING TIME 20 MINUTES**

## INGREDIENTS

2 tbsp sunflower oil
1 onion, chopped
2 large carrots, peeled and chopped
2 sticks of celery, peeled and chopped
1 l / 1 pint 16 fl. oz / 4 cups low-sodium
    chicken stock, hot
2 large, cooked chicken breasts, sliced
1 small bunch of flat-leaf parsley, chopped
Salt and freshly ground black pepper

## METHOD

- Heat the oil in a large saucepan set over a medium heat until hot.
- Add the onion, carrot, celery and a pinch of salt. Sweat for 5 minutes until slightly softened.
- Add the stock and simmer for 10 minutes, then stir in the chicken.
- Cook for a further 5 minutes and season to taste with salt and pepper.
- Stir in the chopped parsley and ladle into soup bowls.

**TOP TIP**
Grate fresh Parmesan over the soup for a delicate finish.

# Spinach Soup

**SERVES 4**

**PREPARATION TIME 10 MINUTES**

**COOKING TIME 15 MINUTES**

## INGREDIENTS

2 tbsp olive oil

1 onion, finely chopped

1 clove of garlic, minced

300 g / 11 oz / 6 cups baby spinach, washed

750 ml / 1 pint 6 fl. oz / 3 cups vegetable
    stock, hot

150 ml / 5 fl. oz / ⅔ cup semi-skimmed milk

75 ml / 3 fl. oz / ⅓ cup double (heavy) cream

a small handful of micro salad, to garnish

salt and freshly ground black pepper

## METHOD

- Heat the oil in a large saucepan set
  over a medium heat until hot.

- Add the onion, garlic and a pinch
  of salt, sweating for 5 minutes
  until softened.

- Add the spinach, stir well and cover
  with the stock and milk. Cook until
  simmering and then continue to
  cook steadily for a further 5 minutes.

- Add the cream, stir well and cook
  over a high heat for 2 minutes.
  Blend with a stick blender until
  completely smooth.

- Season to taste with salt and pepper
  and ladle into bowls. Garnish with
  micro salad on top before serving.

**TOP TIP**
Try substituting half of
the spinach for kale or
Swiss chard.

# Chicken Salad

SERVES 4

PREPARATION TIME 10 MINUTES

COOKING TIME 15 MINUTES

## INGREDIENTS

2 tbsp sunflower oil
2 large, skinless chicken breasts, sliced
75 ml / 3 fl. oz / ⅓ cup extra-virgin olive oil
2 tbsp white wine vinegar
2 large oranges, segmented
1 head of radicchio, roughly chopped
1 red onion, finely sliced
a bunch of flat-leaf parsley, chopped
salt and freshly ground black pepper

## METHOD

- Heat the sunflower oil in a large frying pan set over a moderate heat until hot.

- Season the chicken with salt and pepper and fry for 8–10 minutes, turning occasionally, until golden and cooked through.

- Meanwhile, whisk together the olive oil, vinegar and seasoning in a bowl to make a quick dressing.

- Add the orange, radicchio, onion and parsley, tossing well to coat. Once the chicken is cooked, add it to the bowl and toss with the other ingredients.

- Lift onto plates and serve.

**TOP TIP**
Use a pair of tongs to quickly and easily turn the chicken in the pan.

# Chicken and Mango Salad

**SERVES 4**

**PREPARATION TIME 10 MINUTES**

**COOKING TIME 10 MINUTES**

## INGREDIENTS

55 ml / 2 fl. oz / ¼ cup sunflower oil

2 cloves of garlic, minced

1 tbsp sesame seeds

½ tsp chilli (chili) flakes

2 large, skinless chicken breasts, sliced

2 tbsp white wine vinegar

1 tsp Dijon mustard

1 tsp honey

75 ml / 3 fl. oz / ⅓ cup olive oil

100 g / 3 ½ oz / 2 cups baby spinach, washed

1 mango, pitted and sliced

1 small cucumber, sliced

salt and freshly ground black pepper

## METHOD

- Stir together the sunflower oil, garlic, sesame seeds, chilli flakes and seasoning in a mixing bowl. Add the chicken and toss well to coat.

- Heat a large frying pan over a moderate heat until hot. Pan-fry the chicken for 7–8 minutes, turning once, until golden.

- Whisk together the white wine vinegar, mustard, honey and a little seasoning in a small bowl. Whisk in the oil in a slow, steady stream until you have a thickened dressing.

- Dress the spinach, mango and cucumber with the dressing, tossing well. Lift onto plates and top with the chicken before serving.

**TOP TIP**

Make sure the chicken slices are about the same size to ensure even cooking.

# Turkey Salad

**SERVES 4**

**PREPARATION TIME 15 MINUTES**

**COOKING TIME 10 MINUTES**

## INGREDIENTS

½ tsp paprika
½ tsp ground cumin
¼ tsp caster (superfine) sugar
½ lemon, juiced
2 turkey escalopes, thinly sliced
2 tbsp olive oil
1 iceberg lettuce, shredded
½ cucumber, peeled, seeded and cut into
     thin batons
a small bunch of flat-leaf parsley, chopped
a small handful of mint leaves, chopped
1 Granny Smith apple, cored and thinly sliced
salt and freshly ground black pepper

## METHOD

- Whisk together the paprika, cumin, sugar, lemon juice and seasoning in a mixing bowl. Add the turkey and toss well to coat.

- Heat the oil in a large frying pan set over a moderate heat until hot. Add the turkey and fry for 6–7 minutes, turning occasionally, until golden and cooked through.

- Toss together the lettuce, half of the cucumber batons and the parsley. Lift onto plates and top with the chopped mint and then the turkey.

- Garnish with the remaining cucumber and the slices of apple on top before serving.

**TOP TIP**
Pound the escalopes then slice and marinate for faster cooking times.

# Duck Salad

## METHOD

- Divide the duck, chicory leaves, rocket and spinach among four serving plates. Scatter with the pomegranate seeds.
- Whisk together the walnut oil, olive oil, pomegranate molasses, balsamic vinegar and seasoning in a small bowl for a quick dressing.
- Spoon the dressing over the salad and top with the flaked almonds, and a little more black pepper before serving.

## SERVES 4

## PREPARATION TIME 15 MINUTES

## COOKING TIME 5 MINUTES

## INGREDIENTS

2 small smoked duck breasts, thinly sliced
2 heads of chicory (endive), leaves separated
100 g / 3 ½ oz / 2 cups rocket (arugula)
a small handful of baby spinach
1 pomegranate, seeds removed
55 ml / 2 fl. oz / ¼ cup walnut oil
2 tbsp olive oil
2 tbsp pomegranate molasses
1 tbsp balsamic vinegar
55 g / 2 oz / ½ cup flaked (slivered) almonds
salt and freshly ground black pepper

**TOP TIP**
Substitute the walnut oil for sunflower and omit the almonds for nut allergies.

# Parma Ham and Fig Salad

## METHOD

- Toss together the cherry tomatoes, chives, lettuce, figs and a little seasoning. Add the Parma ham and toss again briefly.
- Lift the salad onto serving plates and drizzle with olive oil. Serve with Melba toasts on the side.

## SERVES 4

## PREPARATION TIME 15 MINUTES

## INGREDIENTS

150 g / 5 oz / 1 cup cherry tomatoes, halved
a large bunch of chives, snipped
½ head of curly lettuce, washed and torn
4 ripe figs, quartered
225 g / 8 oz / 1 ½ cups Parma ham, sliced
75 ml / 3 fl. oz / ⅓ cup extra-virgin olive oil
Melba toasts, to serve
salt and freshly ground black pepper

**TOP TIP**

Smoked meats such as honey-glazed ham or pastrami can be used in this salad.

# Beef Salad

## METHOD

- Heat a heavy-based frying pan over a high heat until it starts to smoke. Rub the steak with the groundnut oil and season with plenty of salt and pepper.
- Pan-fry for 9–10 minutes, turning after 5 minutes. Remove the steak to a plate and cover loosely with aluminium foil, leaving it to rest for at least 5 minutes.
- Meanwhile, whisk together the sunflower oil, rice wine vinegar, lime juice and soy sauce in a large mixing bowl. Add the sliced vegetables and the parsley, tossing well to coat.
- Slice the steak, add to the bowl and toss briefly before lifting into bowls and serving.

**SERVES 4**

**PREPARATION TIME 15 MINUTES**

**COOKING TIME 15 MINUTES**

## INGREDIENTS

450 g / 1 lb sirloin steak, trimmed
2 tbsp groundnut oil
75 ml / 3 fl. oz / ⅓ cup sunflower oil
2 tbsp rice wine vinegar
1 tbsp lime juice
1 tbsp dark soy sauce
225 g / 8 oz / 1 ½ cups cherry tomatoes, sliced
2 large yellow peppers, thinly sliced
2 large red peppers, thinly sliced
4 heads of pak choi (bok choy), thinly sliced
a bunch of flat-leaf parsley, chopped
salt and freshly ground black pepper

**TOP TIP**
Add 1 tbsp of honey to the dressing for a sweeter version.

# Prawn and Pea Salad

**SERVES 4**

**PREPARATION TIME 10 MINUTES**

**COOKING TIME 10 MINUTES**

## INGREDIENTS

2 tbsp butter

4 spring onions (scallions), sliced

1 little gem lettuce, chopped

350 g / 12 oz / 3 cups fresh peas

500 ml / 18 fl. oz / 2 cups vegetable stock, hot

450 g / 1 lb / 3 cups prawns (shrimp), peeled
    and deveined

1 small handful of flat-leaf parsley,
    finely chopped

Salt and freshly ground black pepper

## METHOD

- Melt the butter in a casserole dish set
  over a medium heat until hot.

- Add the spring onion and sweat for
  3 minutes, stirring occasionally.
  Add the lettuce, peas and stock,
  stirring well.

- Cook for a further 3 minutes
  before stirring in the prawns and
  parsley. Cover with a lid and cook
  over a slightly reduced heat until
  the prawns are pink and tender
  to the touch.

- Season to taste with salt and pepper
  before serving in bowls.

**TOP TIP**

Try swirling in a drizzle of cream just before serving for a touch of luxury.

# Salmon Salad

**SERVES 4**

**PREPARATION TIME 10 MINUTES**

**COOKING TIME 10 MINUTES**

## INGREDIENTS

2 tbsp olive oil

1 red chilli (chili), seeded and sliced

2 large, skinless salmon fillets

400 g / 14 oz / 2 cups plain yoghurt

½ lemon, juiced

1 clove of garlic, minced

¼ tsp caster (superfine) sugar

a small bunch of chives

100 g / 3 ½ oz / 1 cup broad (fava)
    beans, shelled

55 g / 2 oz / 1 cup purple salad leaves

150 g / 5 oz / 3 cups rocket (arugula)

salt and freshly ground black pepper

## METHOD

- Preheat the grill to hot.
- Whisk together the olive, chilli and seasoning in a shallow bowl. Add the salmon and coat in the oil.
- Grill for 7–8 minutes, turning once, until the flesh if firm yet springy to the touch.
- Blitz together the yoghurt, lemon juice, garlic, sugar, chives and seasoning in a food processor to make a quick dressing.
- Arrange the broad beans, purple salad leaves and rocket in bowls. Flake the salmon and sit on top, serving with the yoghurt dressing on the side.

**TOP TIP**
Remember to pick through the salmon for any pin-bones before serving.

# Mackerel Salad with Beetroot and Potatoes

**SERVES 4**

**PREPARATION TIME 10 MINUTES**

**COOKING TIME 20 MINUTES**

## INGREDIENTS

750 g / 1 lb 10 oz / 5 cups waxy potatoes, peeled and diced

75 ml / 3 fl. oz / ⅓ cup olive oil

2 tbsp white wine vinegar

1 tsp wholegrain mustard

200 g / 7 oz / 4 cups mixed salad leaves

300 g / 11 oz / 2 cups cooked beetroot in juice, drained and halved

4 smoked mackerel fillets, skinned

1 small red onion, thinly sliced

a few sprigs of oregano

salt and freshly ground black pepper

## METHOD

- Cook the potato in a large saucepan of salted, boiling water for 15–18 minutes until tender to the point of a knife.

- Meanwhile, combine the olive oil, vinegar, mustard and seasoning in a clean jam jar. Seal with a lid and shake well until combined.

- Drain the potato and leave to cool briefly.

- Divide the mixed salad leaves between plates and top with the potato and beetroot. Break apart the mackerel fillets and place on top of the salad along with the red onion.

- Spoon over some of the dressing and garnish with sprigs of oregano and a little more ground pepper before serving.

**TOP TIP**

Give the dressing a quick shake just before serving.

# Potato Salad

## METHOD

- Cook the potatoes in a large saucepan of salted, boiling water for 12–15 minutes until soft to the point of a knife.
- Drain well and leave to cool briefly.
- Combine with the cucumber, olive oil and seasoning in a mixing bowl. Stir for 1 minute until the edges of the potato start to break down.
- Spoon onto plates and garnish with chives.

## SERVES 4

## PREPARATION TIME 10 MINUTES

## COOKING TIME 20 MINUTES

## INGREDIENTS

750 g / 1 lb 10 oz / 5 cups new potatoes, peeled and thickly sliced
½ cucumber, halved and sliced
55 ml / 2 fl. oz / ¼ cup olive oil
a small bunch of chives, snipped
salt and freshly ground black pepper

**TOP TIP**
Stir through 1 tbsp of wholegrain mustard along with the olive oil.

# Waldorf Salad

## METHOD

- Whisk together the yoghurt, mayonnaise, lemon juice, warm water and seasoning in a bowl.
- Add the walnuts, apple, grapes and celery, stirring well to coat in the dressing.
- Arrange the lettuce leaves in serving plates and top with the dressed mixture of walnuts, apples, grapes and celery.

## SERVES 4

## PREPARATION TIME 15 MINUTES

## INGREDIENTS

55 g / 2 oz / ½ cup plain yoghurt
55 g / 2 oz / ½ cup mayonnaise
2 tbsp lemon juice
2 tbsp warm water
150 g / 5 oz / 1 ½ cups walnut halves
2 Braeburn apples, cored and diced
225 g / 8 oz / 1 ½ cups red seedless grapes, halved
4 sticks of celery, peeled and sliced
2 heads of butter lettuce, leaves separated
salt and freshly ground black pepper

**TOP TIP**
Try this classic salad with washed kale leaves for a modern version.

# Fast Lunches and Little Bites

# Spring Rolls with Chilli Sauce

## SERVES 4

## PREPARATION TIME 20 MINUTES

## COOKING TIME 10 MINUTES

## INGREDIENTS

1 l / 1 pint 16 fl. oz / 4 cups vegetable oil, for
    deep-frying
100 g / 3 ½ oz / 2 cups beansprouts
2 carrots, peeled and grated
1 onion, finely sliced
1 red pepper, seeded and thinly sliced
1 yellow pepper, seeded and thinly sliced
a small bunch of coriander
    (cilantro), chopped
2 tbsp dark soy sauce
2 tbsp rice wine vinegar
8 spring roll wrappers, kept under a
    damp cloth
1 large egg white
150 g / 5 oz / ⅔ cup sweet chilli (chili) sauce,
    to serve

## METHOD

- Heat the oil in a large, heavy-based
  saucepan to 180°C / 350F.
- Toss together the vegetables and
  coriander with the soy sauce and
  vinegar in a mixing bowl.
- Working one by one, brush the edges
  of the spring rolls wrappers with a
  little beaten egg white. Arrange the
  vegetable mixture in the centre of the
  wrappers. Bring the edges over the
  filling and roll tightly to secure.
- Deep-fry, in batches, until golden
  brown and crisp; 3–4 minutes.
- Drain on kitchen paper and serve
  with the chilli sauce for dipping.

**TOP TIP**
Flip the spring rolls halfway through deep-frying to brown evenly all over.

# Quick Crostini

## METHOD

- Preheat the oven to 200°C (180°C fan) / 400F / gas 6. Brush the slices of baguette with a little olive oil on both sides.

- Bake in the oven for 4–5 minutes, turning once, until golden on both sides. Remove to a wire rack to cool.

- Toss any remaining oil with the sliced tomatoes and a little seasoning.

- Spoon on top of the toasted baguette slices and top with olives and shave over some Parmesan.

- Garnish with basil leaves and spring onions before serving.

**SERVES 4**

**PREPARATION TIME 15 MINUTES**

**COOKING TIME 5 MINUTES**

## INGREDIENTS

1 baguette, cut into slices

110 ml / 4 fl. oz / ½ cup extra-virgin olive oil

4 plum or Roma tomatoes, sliced

150 g / 5 oz / 1 cup sliced black olives

100 g / 3 ½ oz / 1 cup Parmesan

a small bunch of basil leaves

2 spring onions (scallions), finely sliced

salt and freshly ground black pepper

**TOP TIP**

Drizzle the crostini with a little balsamic vinegar for a touch of sweetness.

77

# Prawn Tempura with Dips

## METHOD

- Whisk together the sesame oil and soy sauce and set to one side. Heat the vegetable oil in a large, heavy-based saucepan to 180°C / 350F.

- Roughly whisk the sparkling water into the flour and cornflour in a mixing bowl. Add the fish sauce and whisk again briefly.

- Dust the vegetables with a little flour before dipping in the tempura batter and deep-frying, in batches, for 2 minutes until golden and crisp. Remove with a slotted spoon and drain on kitchen paper.

- Dust the prawns with flour before coating in the batter and deep-frying for 3 minutes until golden and crisp. Remove with a slotted spoon and drain on kitchen paper.

- Serve the vegetable and prawn tempura with the dipping sauce.

### SERVES 4

### PREPARATION TIME 10 MINUTES

### COOKING TIME 20 MINUTES

## INGREDIENTS

75 ml / 3 fl. oz / ⅓ cup sesame oil

75 ml / 3 fl. oz / ⅓ cup dark soy sauce

1.25 l / 2 pints 4 fl. oz / 5 cups vegetable oil, for deep-frying

250 ml / 9 fl. oz / 1 cup sparkling water, ice cold

150 g / 5 oz / 1 cup plain (all-purpose) flour, plus extra for dusting

2 tbsp cornflour (cornstarch)

1 tbsp fish sauce

1 large courgette (zucchini), sliced

150 g / 5 oz / 1 ½ cups mangetout

600 g / 1 lb 5 oz / 4 cups prawns (shrimp), peeled and deveined with tails intact

**TOP TIP**

Vegetables such as green beans and peppers are also ideal for tempura.

# Quick Hummus

SERVES 4

PREPARATION TIME 15 MINUTES

## INGREDIENTS

500 g / 1 lb 5 oz / 3 cups canned chickpeas
    (garbanzo beans), drained

150 ml / 5 fl. oz / ⅔ cup water

2 cloves of garlic, minced

1 red chilli (chili), seeded and chopped

2 tbsp tahini paste

1 tsp ground cumin

2 tbsp lemon juice

¼ tsp smoked paprika

65 ml / 2 fl. oz / ¼ cup extra-virgin olive oil

1 small handful of flat-leaf parsley,
    finely chopped

Sliced white bread, to serve

Salt and freshly ground black pepper

## METHOD

- Combine the chickpeas with the water, garlic, chilli, tahini, cumin, lemon juice and smoked paprika in a food processor.

- Blitz until smooth, adding the olive oil once the mixture starts to break up and become smooth.

- Continue to blitz until smooth, seasoning to taste with salt and pepper.

- Spoon into a serving bowl and garnish with chopped parsley, serving with slices of bread.

**TOP TIP**
Leave out the chilli (chili) for a less spicy hummus.

# Chicken and Avocado Panini

**MAKES 4**

**PREPARATION TIME 10 MINUTES**

**COOKING TIME 20 MINUTES**

## INGREDIENTS

8 slices of white sandwich bread
200 g / 7 oz / 2 cups mozzarella, grated
4 cooked chicken breasts, sliced
1 tsp paprika
2 avocados, pitted, peeled and sliced
110 ml / 4 fl. oz / ½ cup olive oil
pickled peppers in vinegar, to serve
salt and freshly ground black pepper

## METHOD

- Preheat a panini press according to the manufacturer's instructions.
- Sprinkle the mozzarella evenly over four slices of bread. Top with slices of chicken, a sprinkling of paprika and then slices of avocado.
- Sit the other slices of bread on top of the avocado and brush the top of the bread with olive oil.
- Sit the oiled-side of two sandwiches directly on the panini press and brush the top side of the sandwiches with some oil. Secure the press and grill the sandwiches until the bread is toasted and golden on both sides.
- Grill the other two paninis in the same way before slicing, stacking and serving with pickled peppers.

**TOP TIP**
Brush the panini press clean between grilling each batch.

# Chicken Goujons with Dipping Sauce

SERVES 4

PREPARATION TIME 10 MINUTES

COOKING TIME 20 MINUTES

## INGREDIENTS

1 l / 1 pint 16 fl. oz / 4 cups vegetable oil, for deep-frying

110 ml / 4 fl. oz / ½ cup warm water

55 g / 2 oz / ¼ cup wholegrain mustard

2 tbsp distilled vinegar

2 tbsp honey

4 large, skinless chicken breasts, trimmed and cut into strips

100 g / 3 ½ oz / ⅔ cup plain (all-purpose) flour

2 large eggs, beaten

150 g / 5 oz / 1 ½ cups golden breadcrumbs

55 g / 2 oz / 1 cup fresh breadcrumbs

55 g / 2 oz / ½ cup Parmesan, grated

a few sprigs of thyme

salt and freshly ground black pepper

## METHOD

- Heat the oil in a large, heavy-based saucepan to 180°C / 350F.

- Blend together the water, mustard, vinegar, honey and seasoning in a food processor until smooth. Pour into pots and cover and chill until needed.

- Pat the slices of chicken dry before dusting in the flour, shaking off the excess and seasoning with salt and pepper. Dip in the beaten egg and dredge in a combination of the breadcrumbs and Parmesan to coat.

- Deep-fry in batches for 4–5 minutes until golden, turning over once.

- Drain on kitchen paper and serve with pots of the dipping sauce and a garnish of thyme.

**TOP TIP**
Add a dollop of mayonnaise when blending the dip for a creamy addition.

# Chicken and Pepper Wraps

## MAKES 4

## PREPARATION TIME 15 MINUTES

## COOKING TIME 15 MINUTES

## INGREDIENTS

2 tbsp olive oil
2 large skinless chicken breasts, sliced
1 large red pepper, seeded and diced
1 large yellow pepper, seeded and diced
75 g / 3 oz / ½ cup sun-dried tomatoes in oil,
    drained and chopped
2 tsp fajita seasoning
2 vine tomatoes, cored and diced
100 g / 3 ½ oz / 2 cups rocket (arugula)
4 white flour tortillas
salt and freshly ground black pepper

## METHOD

- Heat the oil in a frying pan over a moderate heat until hot. Add the chicken and plenty of seasoning, frying for 5 minutes until starting to brown.
- Add the peppers, sun-dried tomato and fajita seasoning, continuing to fry for further 4–5 minutes until the chicken is cooked through.
- Stir in the fresh tomato and season to taste with salt and pepper. Remove from the heat and preheat a dry griddle pan over a moderate heat at the same time.
- Lay the tortillas flat and top with the rocket and then the fried chicken and vegetable mixture.
- Roll the wraps securely and griddle in the hot pan until lightly charred before serving.

**TOP TIP**
A dollop of sour cream or crème fraiche makes an ideal accompaniment to these wraps.

# Beef Sandwich

**MAKES 4**

**PREPARATION TIME 20 MINUTES**

**COOKING TIME 8 MINUTES**

## INGREDIENTS

10 cm (4 in) piece of horseradish,
    peeled and grated
½ lemon, juiced
250 ml / 9 fl. oz / 1 cup whipping cream
1 tbsp sunflower oil
1 tbsp butter
1 large white onion, sliced
450 g / 1 lb / 3 cups roast beef, sliced
4 white rolls, split
salt and freshly ground black pepper

## METHOD

- Combine the grated horseradish with the lemon juice and seasoning in a mixing bowl.

- Briefly whip the cream in a separate bowl until softly peaked.

- Drain the horseradish from the lemon juice and fold into the whipped cream.

- Heat the oil with the butter in a large frying pan set over a medium heat until hot. Add the onion and a pinch of salt, sweating for 5 minutes until soft.

- Fold slices of beef on top of the bottom halves of the rolls. Top with the onions and horseradish cream. Sit the tops of the rolls in place before serving.

**TOP TIP**
Replace the cream with half-fat crème fraiche or fromage frais for a lighter version.

# Club Sandwiches

**MAKES 4**

**PREPARATION TIME 10 MINUTES**

**COOKING TIME 15 MINUTES**

## INGREDIENTS

2 tbsp olive oil

2 small skinless chicken breasts, sliced

12 slices of white bread

150 g / 5 oz / ⅔ cup mayonnaise

75 g / 3 oz / ¾ cup Cheddar, sliced

75 g / 3 oz / ½ cup sliced gherkins in vinegar

½ small head of round lettuce,
   leaves separated

3 vine tomatoes, cored and sliced

4 slices of cooked ham

salt and freshly ground black pepper

## METHOD

- Heat the oil in a large frying pan set over a moderate heat until hot.

- Season the chicken with salt and pepper and fry for 8–10 minutes until golden and cooked through.

- Meanwhile, toast the slices of bread under a hot grill or in a toaster.

- Spread eight of them with mayonnaise and top half of those with cheese and gherkins. Follow with the cooked chicken and then lettuce.

- Place the four slices of toast with mayonnaise on top of the lettuce, mayonnaise-side down. Top those slices of toast with tomato, ham and more lettuce.

- Spread the last four slices of toast with mayonnaise and place them, mayonnaise-side down, on the lettuce.

- Cut in half before serving with any remaining mayonnaise on the side.

**TOP TIP**

Wholemeal or wholegrain bread can be used as an alternative.

# Chilli Nachos

**ERVES 4**

**REPARATION TIME 5 MINUTES**

**OOKING TIME 25 MINUTES**

## INGREDIENTS

- tbsp sunflower oil
- cloves of garlic, minced
- small onion, finely chopped
- tsp paprika
- ½ tsp chilli (chili) powder
- tsp ground cumin
- tsp ground coriander
- 00 g / 14 oz / 2 cups canned chopped tomatoes
- 00 g / 14 oz / 2 cups canned kidney beans, drained
- 50 g / 5 oz / 1 ½ cups grated mozzarella
- 00 g / 7 oz / 4 cups tortilla chips
- 25 g / 8 oz / 1 cup guacamole
- 10 g / 4 oz / ½ cup sour cream
- small bunch of coriander (cilantro), chopped
- alt and freshly ground black pepper

## METHOD

- Heat the oil in a large frying pan set over a moderate heat until hot. Add the garlic and onion and fry for 2 minutes, stirring frequently.

- Add the ground spices and continue to cook for 1 minute, stirring. Stir in the tomatoes, beans and 100 ml / 3 ½ fl. oz / ½ cup of water with half of the mozzarella.

- Cover with a lid and simmer for 15 minutes until the beans are tender. Season to taste and set to one side.

- Preheat the grill to hot. Divide the chips between heatproof bowls and top with the remaining mozzarella. Grill for 1–2 minutes until the mozzarella is melted and bubbling.

- Carefully remove from the grill and top with the chilli. Serve with guacamole, sour cream and coriander on top.

**TOP TIP**

Remember to use oven mitts or a thick cloth to remove the bowls from the grill.

# Camembert Fondue

## METHOD

- Preheat the oven to 200°C (180°C fan) / 400F / gas 6.
- Place the Camembert on a baking tray, in its case, with the top removed. Drizzle with olive oil and stud with rosemary.
- Bake for 10 minutes or until the cheese is melted and gooey.
- Remove from the oven and serve immediately with the bread on the side.

**SERVES 4**

**PREPARATION TIME 5 MINUTES**

**COOKING TIME 10 MINUTES**

## INGREDIENTS

1 wheel of Camembert, in its case
1 tbsp olive oil
2 sprigs of rosemary, chopped
multigrain or fruit bread, to serve

**TOP TIP**

Drizzle the Camembert with honey before baking for a sweet alternative.

# Grilled Courgettes

**SERVES 4**

**PREPARATION TIME 10 MINUTES**

**COOKING TIME 20 MINUTES**

## INGREDIENTS

2 courgettes (zucchinis), sliced
1 yellow courgette (zucchini), sliced
2 baby courgettes (zucchinis), split in half
75 ml / 3 fl. oz / ⅓ cup olive oil
75 ml / 3 fl. oz / ⅓ cup extra-virgin olive oil
2 tbsp balsamic vinegar
100 g / 3 ½ oz / 1 cup feta, crumbled
1 handful of mint leaves, sliced
Salt and freshly ground black pepper

## METHOD

- Preheat a griddle pan over a moderate heat.

- Toss the courgettes in a mixing bowl with olive oil and plenty of salt and pepper.

- Griddle the courgettes in batches until lightly charred and tender to the point of a knife.

- Whisk together the extra-virgin olive oil and balsamic vinegar to make a quick dressing. Season to taste with salt and pepper.

- Arrange the courgettes on a serving plate and top with the feta, mint and dressing.

**TOP TIP**
Add a handful of pomegranate seeds for crunch and sweetness.

# Goats' Cheese and Pea Frittata

## SERVES 4

## PREPARATION TIME 10 MINUTES

## COOKING TIME 20 MINUTES

## INGREDIENTS

2 tbsp unsalted butter

750 g / 1 lb 10 oz / 5 cups floury potatoes, peeled and sliced

8 large eggs, beaten

110 g / 4 oz / ½ cup crème fraiche

250 g / 9 oz / 2 cups fresh peas

a handful of mint leaves

150 g / 5 oz / 1 ½ cups goats' cheese, chopped

salt and freshly ground black pepper

## METHOD

- Preheat the oven to 190°C (170°C fan) / 375F / gas 5. Melt the butter in a cast-iron frying pan set over a moderate heat until hot.

- Add the potatoes in layers, seasoning in between them. Cover the pan with a lid and cook for 2 minutes.

- Beat together the eggs and crème fraiche and pour over the potato. Top with the peas, mint, goats' cheese and seasoning.

- Cover with a lid and bake for 5 minutes. Remove the lid and bake for a further 10 minutes until golden on top.

- Remove from the oven and leave to stand briefly before serving.

**TOP TIP**

Slide a knife around the inside edge of the pan to loosen the frittata.

# 30 Minutes
# or Under

## 30 MINUTES OR UNDER

# Chicken and Bacon Tagliatelle

**SERVES 4**

**PREPARATION TIME 10 MINUTES**

**COOKING TIME 10 MINUTES**

## INGREDIENTS

2 tbsp olive oil

150 g / 5 oz / 1 cup pancetta lardons

2 large cooked chicken breasts, diced

2 cloves of garlic, minced

350 g / 12 oz / 3 cups fresh tagliatelle

55 g / 2 oz / ½ cup Parmesan, grated

a small bunch of flat-leaf parsley, chopped

salt and freshly ground black pepper

## METHOD

- Heat the oil in a large frying pan set over a medium heat until hot. Add the pancetta, chicken and garlic and fry for 3 minutes until lightly golden.

- Cook the tagliatelle in a large saucepan of salted, boiling water for 3 minutes until 'al dente'. Drain well and toss with the chicken and bacon.

- Add the Parmesan and parsley, tossing well. Season to taste with salt and pepper before serving.

**TOP TIP**

Add 1 tbsp of crème fraiche to the pasta when tossing with the chicken.

# Quick Chicken Tikka Masala

**SERVES 4**

**PREPARATION TIME 10 MINUTES**

**COOKING TIME 20 MINUTES**

## INGREDIENTS

2 onions, chopped
6 cloves of garlic, crushed
5 cm (2 in) piece of root ginger, peeled
55 ml / 2 fl. oz / ¼ cup vegetable oil
1 tbsp ground cumin
1 tbsp ground coriander
1 tsp paprika
2 green chillies (chilies), sliced
2 bay leaves
225 g / 8 oz / 1 cup roasted red peppers
4 cooked chicken breasts, diced
200 g / 7 oz / 1 cup passata
250 ml / 9 fl. oz / 1 cup chicken stock
150 ml / 5 fl. oz / ⅔ cup double (heavy) cream
salt and freshly ground black pepper

## METHOD

- Blend together the onion, garlic and ginger in a food processor until paste-like.
- Heat the oil in a large casserole dish or saucepan set over a moderate heat until hot. Add the paste and fry with a little salt and pepper for 3 minutes.
- Stir in the ground spices, green chillies and bay leaves, stirring well. Cook for 2 minutes and then add the roasted red peppers, chicken, passata, stock and cream.
- Simmer for 15 minutes, stirring well, until thickened. Season to taste with salt and pepper before serving.

**TOP TIP**
Try some cubed salmon fillet in this recipe for a quick salmon tikka masala.

# Breaded Chicken Escalope

**SERVES 4**

**PREPARATION TIME 10 MINUTES**

**COOKING TIME 20 MINUTES**

## INGREDIENTS

4 small skinless chicken breasts, pounded out with a tenderiser
55 g / 2 oz / ⅓ cup plain (all-purpose) flour
2 large eggs, beaten
225 g / 8 oz / 1 ½ cups panko breadcrumbs
a small bunch of dill, chopped
2 tbsp sunflower oil
300 g / 10 ½ oz / 2 cups new potatoes
75 g / 3 oz / ⅓ cup mayonnaise
1 lemon, cut into wedges
salt and freshly ground black pepper

## METHOD

- Preheat the oven to 200°C (180°C fan) / 400F / gas 6. Line a large baking tray with a sheet of greaseproof paper.

- Dust the chicken with flour, shaking off any excess, then season.

- Dip in the egg to coat, then dredge in a mixture of the breadcrumbs and some of the chopped dill.

- Arrange on the baking tray and drizzle with oil. Bake for 20 minutes until golden.

- Meanwhile, cook the potatoes in a large saucepan of salted, boiling water for 15–18 minutes until tender to the point of a knife.

- Drain well and stir with the mayonnaise and some lemon juice from one of the wedges in a mixing bowl. Season to taste.

- Serve the breaded escalopes on plates with the potatoes, wedges of lemon and a garnish of dill.

**TOP TIP**
Flip the breaded escalopes after 10 minutes in the oven.

# Jerk Chicken

SERVES 4

PREPARATION TIME 10 MINUTES

COOKING TIME 20 MINUTES

## INGREDIENTS

- 1 tbsp thyme leaves
- 110 g / 4 oz / ½ cup barbecue sauce
- 2 spring onions (scallions), chopped
- 2 limes
- ½ tsp ground allspice
- 1 tbsp dark soy sauce
- 55 ml / 2 fl. oz / ¼ cup vegetable oil
- 2 large cooked chicken breasts, diced
- 200 g / 7 oz / 1 cup canned kidney beans, drained
- 200 g / 7 oz / 1 cup canned white beans, drained
- 1 stick of celery, finely diced
- 1 red pepper, seeded and finely diced
- 1 green pepper, seeded and finely diced
- 350 g / 12 oz / 3 cups cooked long-grain white rice
- a few sprigs of flat-leaf parsley, to garnish
- salt and freshly ground black pepper

## METHOD

- Blend together the thyme leaves, barbecue sauce, spring onions, juice of one lime, allspice, soy sauce and 150 ml / ¼ pt / ⅔ cup of warm water in a blender.

- Heat half of the oil in a casserole dish set over a medium heat until hot. Add the chicken and sauté briefly before adding the beans and the prepared sauce.

- Cover with a lid and simmer for 15 minutes until the beans are tender. Season to taste once ready.

- Meanwhile, heat the remaining oil in a large frying pan set over a moderate heat until hot. Add the celery, diced peppers and a little salt.

- Fry for 2 minutes and then add the rice. Continue to fry over a reduced heat, stirring occasionally, until the rice is piping hot throughout.

- Serve the jerk chicken over the rice with slices from the remaining lime and sprigs of parsley.

**TOP TIP**

Add a couple of dashes of hot sauce for added spice.

# Sausages with Mash and Onion

**SERVES 4**

**PREPARATION TIME 10 MINUTES**

**COOKING TIME 20 MINUTES**

## INGREDIENTS

8 good-quality pork sausages, pricked with a fork

1 tbsp sunflower oil

1 tbsp butter

1 white onion, finely sliced

1 red onion, finely sliced

½ tsp caster (superfine) sugar

250 ml / 9 fl. oz / 1 cup beef stock

110 ml / 4 fl. oz / ½ cup red wine

1 tbsp arrowroot, mixed with 1 tbsp water

900 g / 2 lb / 5 cups cooked mashed potato

salt and freshly ground black pepper

## METHOD

- Preheat the grill to a moderate heat. Arrange the sausages on a tray and grill for 10–12 minutes, turning occasionally, until golden all over.

- Meanwhile, heat together the oil and butter in a saucepan set over a medium heat until hot. Add the onions, a pinch of salt and the sugar. Sweat for 5 minutes, stirring occasionally, until softened.

- Add the stock and wine and increase the heat until boiling. Reduce to a simmer and cook for a further 5 minutes. Thicken it by whisking some of the arrowroot paste into the simmering gravy. Season to taste with salt and pepper.

- Reheat the mashed potato in a microwave on a high setting. Spoon into dishes and top with the sausages and gravy before serving.

**TOP TIP**

Mash 2 tbsp of butter and cream into the potato before reheating.

# Sausage Gnocchi

**SERVES 4**

**PREPARATION TIME 10 MINUTES**

**COOKING TIME 15 MINUTES**

## INGREDIENTS

2 tbsp olive oil
150 g / 5 oz / 2 cups button mushrooms, sliced
300 g / 10 ½ oz / 2 cups smoked sausage,
    sliced
450 g / 1 lb / 4 cups cooked gnocchi
150 ml / 5 fl. oz / ⅔ cup vegetable stock
75 g / 3 oz / ¾ cup Parmesan, grated
a small bunch of flat-leaf parsley, chopped
salt and freshly ground black pepper

## METHOD

- Heat the olive oil in a large sauté pan set over a moderate heat until hot.

- Add the mushrooms, sausage and a pinch of salt and pepper. Sauté for 5–6 minutes until the mushrooms start to brown.

- Add the gnocchi and stock. Cook for a further 5 minutes, until the gnocchi is piping hot.

- Stir in the Parmesan and parsley. Season to taste with salt and pepper before serving.

**TOP TIP**

Stir in some cubed goats' cheese instead of Parmesan for a creamy finish.

# Mustard Pork Chops

**SERVES 4**

**PREPARATION TIME 10 MINUTES**

**COOKING TIME 20 MINUTES**

## INGREDIENTS

2 tbsp sunflower oil

2 tbsp wholegrain mustard

1 tbsp honey

4 bone-in centre cut pork chops, trimmed

2 tbsp olive oil

2 cloves of garlic, minced

2 red peppers, seeded and sliced

1 small head of broccoli, prepared into florets

300 g / 10 ½ oz / 2 cups cooked new potatoes

salt and freshly ground black pepper

## METHOD

- Preheat the oven to 200°C (180°C fan) / 400F / gas 6.

- Whisk together the sunflower oil, mustard, honey and seasoning in a shallow dish. Add the pork chops and coat in the marinade.

- Arrange in a roasting tray and roast for 12–15 minutes until the pork chops register at least 66°C / 155F on a meat thermometer.

- As the pork chops roast, heat the oil in a large frying pan set over a medium heat until hot. Add the garlic and peppers, frying for 2 minutes.

- Add the broccoli and potatoes. Cover the pan with a lid and cook for 5 minutes until the broccoli is tender. Season to taste with salt and pepper.

- Serve the roast pork chops over the vegetables.

**TOP TIP**

Leave the pork chops to marinate for up to 1 hour in the fridge.

# Beef Fajitas

## METHOD

- Heat the oil in a large frying pan set over a moderate heat until hot. Season the steak and fry in the hot oil for 4 minutes, turning once.

- Add the peppers and onion and continue to fry for 4 minutes, tossing occasionally. Add the fajita seasoning, stir well and fry for a further 3 minutes over a reduced heat.

- Heat a dry frying pan over a moderate heat until hot. Dry-fry the tortillas for 20–30 seconds, flipping once, until soft and warmed through.

- Fill with the beef and vegetables and serve with the sour cream garnished with paprika as well as the salsa.

## SERVES 4

## PREPARATION TIME 10 MINUTES

## COOKING TIME 20 MINUTES

## INGREDIENTS

2 tbsp sunflower oil

500 g / 1 lb 5 oz piece of sirloin steak, sliced

1 large red pepper, seeded and sliced

1 large yellow pepper, seeded and sliced

1 onion, finely sliced

2 tsp fajita seasoning

8 flour tortillas

150 g / 5 oz / ⅔ cup sour cream, to serve

a pinch of paprika

150 g / 5 oz / ⅔ cup salsa, to serve

salt and freshly ground black pepper

**TOP TIP**
Wet each tortilla with a sprinkle of water to prevent them from sticking.

# Grilled Steak

## METHOD

- Cook the potatoes in a large saucepan of salted, boiling water for 15 minutes. Preheat the grill to hot.

- Heat the oil in a cast-iron frying pan set over a high heat until hot. Pat the steaks dry and season generously with salt and pepper.

- Lay them carefully in the hot pan and cook, undisturbed, for 4 minutes. Flip and cook for a further 4 minutes, adding the butter and rosemary after a couple of minutes.

- Remove the steaks from the pan and reduce the heat under the pan to low. Cover the steaks with aluminium foil and leave them to rest for at least 5 minutes.

- Drain the potatoes well and add to the hot pan, frying with a little salt and pepper, until golden at the edges.

- Serve the steaks with the potatoes and tomato ketchup on the side.

## SERVES 4

## PREPARATION TIME 5 MINUTES

## COOKING TIME 25 MINUTES

## INGREDIENTS

300 g / 10 ½ oz / 2 cups new potatoes
1 tbsp groundnut oil
2 x 250 g / 9 oz sirloin steaks, trimmed
1 tbsp butter, cubed
2 sprigs of rosemary
150 g / 5 oz / ⅔ cup tomato ketchup, to serve
salt and freshly ground black pepper

**TOP TIP**
Remember to baste the steaks with the melted butter.

# Steak Burger with Rocket

MAKES 4

PREPARATION TIME 15 MINUTES

COOKING TIME 10 MINUTES

## INGREDIENTS

110 g / 4 oz / 1 cup Gorgonzola, cubed

75 g / 3 oz / ⅓ cup sour cream

2 tbsp vegetable oil

4 small sirloin steaks

4 semolina burger buns

1 small cucumber, thinly sliced

2 large yellow tomatoes, finely sliced

2 tbsp flat-leaf parsley, chopped

100 g / 3 ½ oz / 2 cups rocket (arugula)

55 g / 2 oz / 1 cup alfalfa sprouts

salt and freshly ground black pepper

## METHOD

- Mash the Gorgonzola with a fork and stir together with the sour cream.

- Heat the oil in a large frying pan set over a high heat until hot. Season the steaks and fry for 4 minutes, undisturbed. Flip and cook for a further 4 minutes until firm yet slightly springy to the touch.

- Remove them from the pan and cover loosely with foil, letting them rest for 5 minutes. Slice into strips.

- Slice each bun in half and spread both halves with the Gorgonzola cream. Top with slices of cucumber and tomato, the sliced steak, parsley, rocket and sprouts. Place the bun lid on top and secure in place with a wooden skewer.

**TOP TIP**

Let the steaks cook for a couple more minutes for well-done meat.

# Spaghetti Bolognese

**SERVES 4**

**PREPARATION TIME 5 MINUTES**

**COOKING TIME 25 MINUTES**

## INGREDIENTS

2 tbsp olive oil
1 onion, finely chopped
2 cloves of garlic, minced
1 carrot, peeled and finely diced
450 g / 1 lb / 3 cups beef mince, 20% fat
400 g / 14 oz / 2 cups canned
    chopped tomatoes
350 g / 12 oz / 3 cups spaghetti
55 g / 2 oz / ½ cup Parmesan
a few sprigs of flat-leaf parsley, to garnish
salt and freshly ground black pepper

## METHOD

- Heat the oil in a large saucepan or casserole dish set over a medium heat until hot. Add the onion, garlic, carrot and a pinch of seasoning, sweating for 5 minutes.

- Increase the heat and add the beef mince, browning well all over and breaking it up with a wooden spoon. Stir in the chopped tomatoes, cover with a lid and cook over a reduced heat for 15 minutes.

- Meanwhile, cook the spaghetti in a large saucepan of salted, boiling water until 'al dente'; 8–10 minutes.

- Drain the spaghetti, reserving a cup of the cooking water and toss with the meat sauce. Add some of the cooking water to loosen, tossing and lifting the spaghetti with tongs. Season to taste with salt and pepper.

- Lift into bowls and grate over some Parmesan. Garnish with parsley before serving.

**TOP TIP**
For a looser sauce, add half a cup of beef stock to the sauce.

# Thai Beef Stir-fry

SERVES 4

PREPARATION TIME 10 MINUTES

COOKING TIME 10 MINUTES

## INGREDIENTS

2 tbsp fish sauce

55 ml / 2 fl. oz / ¼ cup light soy sauce

1 lime, juiced

2 tbsp soft light brown sugar

400 g / 14 oz sirloin steak, sliced

55 ml / 2 fl. oz / ¼ cup groundnut oil

2 red chillies (chilies), sliced

4 sticks of celery, sliced

350 g / 12 oz / 3 cups cooked egg noodles

110 g / 4 oz / 1 cup green (string) beans, chopped

1 small handful of mint leaves

1 small bunch of coriander (cilantro), torn

## METHOD

- Stir together the fish sauce, soy sauce, lime juice, sugar and 55 ml / 2 fl. oz / ¼ cup of warm water in a small bowl. Add the steak, stirring well to coat.

- Heat the oil in a large wok set over a high heat until hot. Remove the steak from the marinade and add it to the wok, stir-frying for 2 minutes.

- Add the chillies and celery, continuing to fry for a further 2 minutes.

- Add the cooked noodles, stirring and tossing for 2 minutes. Add the reserved marinade and cook for 1 minute, stirring frequently.

- Stir in the chopped green beans and cook for a further minute.

- Lift into bowls and garnish with the herbs before serving.

**TOP TIP**

Take care when adding the steak to the hot oil in the wok as it may spit initially.

# Quick Hawaiian Pizza

**MAKES 4 MINI PIZZAS**

**PREPARATION TIME 10 MINUTES**

**COOKING TIME 10 MINUTES**

## INGREDIENTS

4 small naan breads
2 tbsp olive oil
150 g / 5 oz / ⅔ cup sun-dried tomato paste
300 g / 10 ½ oz / 1 ½ cups canned pineapple
    chunks, drained
8 slices of Parma ham, torn
100 g / 3 ½ oz / 1 cup mozzarella, grated
2 spring onion (scallions), finely sliced
salt and freshly ground black pepper

## METHOD

- Preheat the oven to 220°C (200°C fan) / 425F / gas 7.
- Brush the naan breads with olive oil and top with teaspoons of the sun-dried tomato paste, chunks of pineapple and slices of ham.
- Sprinkle over the cheese and season with salt and pepper. Place onto a large baking tray lined with greaseproof paper.
- Bake for 5–7 minutes until the bread is golden and the cheese has melted.
- Remove from the oven and serve with a garnish of spring onion on top.

**TOP TIP**
Try substituting the sun-dried tomato paste for basil pesto.

# Lamb Chops

## METHOD

- Preheat a griddle pan over a moderate heat until hot.
- Rub the lamb chops with the spices and seasoning. Drizzle with a little olive oil and cook, in batches, in the griddle pan for 3 minutes on both sides for medium meat.
- Remove to a tray and cover with aluminium foil, leaving them to rest for at least 5 minutes.
- Toss together the remaining olive oil, beansprouts, tomatoes, red onion, coriander, lime juice and seasoning in a mixing bowl.
- Serve the salad with the lamb chops and tortilla chips on the side.

SERVES 4

PREPARATION TIME 15 MINUTES

COOKING TIME 15 MINUTES

## INGREDIENTS

bone-in lamb chops, trimmed
tsp ground cumin
tsp paprika
½ tsp dried oregano
5 ml / 2 fl. oz / ¼ cup olive oil
00 g / 3 ½ oz / 2 cups beansprouts
vine tomatoes, cored and diced
½ red onion, finely sliced
bunch of coriander (cilantro), chopped
lime, juiced
ortilla chips, to serve
alt and freshly ground black pepper

**TOP TIP**
If using a meat thermometer, the chops should register at 71°C/160F for medium.

# Tuna and Olive Pasta

## SERVES 4

## PREPARATION TIME 10 MINUTES

## COOKING TIME 15 MINUTES

## INGREDIENTS

450 g / 1 lb / 4 cups rigatoni
2 tbsp olive oil
1 clove of garlic, minced
300 g / 10 ½ oz / 1 ½ cups canned tuna
    steak, drained
400 ml / 14 fl. oz / 1 ⅔ cups passata
150 g / 5 oz / 1 cup Kalamata olives
a small bunch of basil, sliced
1 tbsp baby capers in brine, drained
salt and freshly ground black pepper

## METHOD

- Cook the pasta in a large saucepan of salted, boiling water until 'al dente'; 8–10 minutes.

- Meanwhile, heat the olive oil in a large saucepan set over a moderate heat until hot.

- Add the garlic and fry for 30 seconds, adding the tuna and passata. Stir well and simmer for 5 minutes.

- Add the olives, stir well and season to taste.

- Drain the pasta when ready and tip into the sauce, stirring and tossing to coat in the sauce.

- Spoon onto a platter and garnish with basil and capers before serving.

**TOP TIP**
If the sauce is a little dry, add some cooking liquid from the pasta to loosen it.

# Seared Salmon

**SERVES 4**

**PREPARATION TIME 10 MINUTES**

**COOKING TIME 15 MINUTES**

## INGREDIENTS

4 salmon steaks, pin-boned
55 ml / 2 fl. oz / ¼ cup olive oil
350 g / 12 oz / 3 cups green (string) beans
75 ml / 3 fl. oz / ⅓ cup balsamic vinegar
1 pomegranate, halved with seeds removed
a small handful of mint leaves
salt and freshly ground black pepper

## METHOD

- Preheat the oven to 200°C (180°C fan) / 400F / gas 6.

- Drizzle the salmon with olive oil and season generously with salt and pepper. Arrange in a roasting dish or on a baking tray. Roast for 12–14 minutes until the flesh is firm to the touch.

- Meanwhile, cook the beans in a large saucepan of salted, boiling water for 3 minutes until tender. Drain and refresh briefly in iced water.

- Stir together the balsamic vinegar and pomegranate seeds in a mixing bowl. Season with salt and pepper.

- Arrange the green beans and mint in serving dishes. Top with the salmon steaks and spoon over the pomegranate seeds and balsamic vinegar before serving.

**TOP TIP**

Try this dish with halibut or cod steaks instead of salmon.

# Pan-fried Scallops

## METHOD

- Whip together the cream cheese, crème fraiche, chives, garlic and seasoning in a mixing bowl. Cover and chill until needed.

- Heat the sunflower oil in a large frying pan set over a moderate heat until hot. Pat the scallops dry and season with salt and pepper.

- Fry in the oil for 2–3 minutes until browned underneath. Flip carefully and fry for a further 1–2 minutes until golden on both sides.

- Lift the scallops onto serving plates and serve with a quenelle of the cream cheese. Garnish with the diced pepper, pine nuts, olive oil, oregano and salad leaves.

## SERVES 4

## PREPARATION TIME 15 MINUTES

## COOKING TIME 10 MINUTES

## INGREDIENTS

150 g / 5 oz / ⅔ cup cream cheese
110 g / 4 oz / ½ cup crème fraiche
a small bunch of chives, finely chopped
1 clove of garlic, minced
2 tbsp sunflower oil
12 queen scallops, with roe removed
2 tbsp butter
1 red pepper, seeded and finely diced
55 g / 2 oz / ½ cup pine nuts, toasted
75 ml / 3 fl. oz / ⅓ cup extra-virgin olive oil
2 tbsp oregano
55 g / 2 oz / 1 cup mixed salad leaves
salt and freshly ground black pepper

**TOP TIP**

Use a couple of dessert spoons to shape the cream cheese mixture.

# Crusted Cod

SERVES 4

PREPARATION TIME 10 MINUTES

COOKING TIME 15 MINUTES

## INGREDIENTS

175 g / 6 oz / 1 cup couscous
1 red chilli (chili), finely chopped
500 ml / 18 fl. oz / 2 cups semi-skimmed milk
1 bay leaf
4 skinless cod fillets
55 ml / 2 fl. oz / ¼ cup olive oil
3 spring onions (scallions), roughly sliced
a small bunch of chervil, torn
salt and freshly ground black pepper

## METHOD

- Preheat the grill to a moderate heat. Place the couscous and chilli in a heatproof bowl and cover with boiling water. Cover the bowl tightly with cling film and set to one side for 5 minutes.

- Warm the milk with the bay leaf in a shallow saucepan set over a medium heat. Once the milk starts to simmer, position the cod in the hot milk and cover with a lid. Cook for 5–6 minutes until the cod is firm yet springy to the touch.

- Fluff the couscous with a fork and season with salt and plenty of black pepper. Add the olive oil and stir well.

- Remove the cod from the poaching liquid and pat dry. Top with the couscous, packing it onto the fillets with your hands.

- Arrange on a tray and grill for 2–3 minutes until the crust starts to brown.

- Place the sliced spring onion and some of the torn chervil on serving plates. Spoon over some of the poaching milk and sit the crusted cod on top. Serve with a garnish of the remaining chervil before serving.

**TOP TIP**

Make sure to remove any pin-bones from the cod when preparing.

# Spaghetti with Prawns and Chilli

**SERVES 4**

**PREPARATION TIME 10 MINUTES**

**COOKING TIME 12 MINUTES**

## INGREDIENTS

450 g / 1 lb / 4 cups spaghetti

2 tbsp olive oil

2 cloves of garlic, minced

2 red chillies (chilies), seeded and chopped

½ tsp paprika

450 g / 1 lb / 3 cups king prawns, peeled and deveined

200 g / 7 oz / 1 cup canned chopped tomatoes

a small bunch of dill, finely chopped

½ lemon, juiced

salt and freshly ground black pepper

## METHOD

- Cook the spaghetti in a large saucepan of salted, boiling water until 'al dente'; 8–10 minutes.

- Heat the oil in a large saucepan set over a moderate heat until hot. Add the garlic, chilli and a little salt, frying for 1 minute.

- Stir in the paprika and add the prawns. Fry for 3 minutes, stirring occasionally, until the prawns are pink. Stir in the chopped tomatoes, dill and lemon juice.

- Cook over a reduced heat for a further 2 minutes, stirring from time to time. Season to taste with salt and pepper and set the pan to one side.

- Drain the spaghetti, reserving a cup of the cooking water. Toss with the prawns, lifting the spaghetti with a pair of tongs to coat in the sauce. Add a little of the reserved cooking liquid to loosen the sauce.

- Season to taste with salt and pepper before lifting into bowls and serving.

**TOP TIP**
This recipe can be made with gluten-free pasta for those with gluten or wheat allergies.

# Vegetable Curry

**SERVES 4**

**PREPARATION TIME 10 MINUTES**

**COOKING TIME 20 MINUTES**

## INGREDIENTS

2 tbsp sunflower oil
1 tbsp mild curry powder
1 courgette (zucchini), sliced
2 carrots, peeled and sliced
1 white onion, chopped
225 g / 8 oz / 2 cups green (string)
   beans, halved
150 g / 5 oz / 2 cups chestnut mushrooms,
   halved
1 small head of broccoli, prepared into florets
150 g / 5 oz / 1 cup baby sweetcorn
1 red pepper, seeded and sliced
500 ml / 18 fl. oz / 2 cups vegetable stock
250 ml / 9 fl. oz / 1 cup coconut milk
100 g / 3 ½ oz / 2 cups baby spinach, washed
salt and freshly ground black pepper

## METHOD

- Heat the oil in a casserole dish set over a medium heat until hot. Add the curry powder and fry for 30 seconds.

- Add the courgette, carrot, onion, beans, mushroom, broccoli, sweetcorn, pepper and stir well.

- Cover with the stock and coconut milk. Simmer for 10–15 minutes until the vegetables are tender.

- Stir in the spinach and cook for a further 2 minutes until wilted. Season to taste with salt and pepper.

- Ladle into bowls and serve.

**TOP TIP**
Serve this curry with bowls of brown or basmati rice on the side.

# Red Pepper Risotto

## METHOD

- Heat the oil in a large saucepan set over a medium heat until hot. Add the peppers, leek, garlic and a little salt, sweating for 5 minutes.

- Stir in the chicken, rice and infused stock. Cook at a simmer for 10 minutes, stirring frequently, until the rice is soft and piping hot.

- Stir through the Parmesan and season to taste with salt and pepper. Spoon into bowls and serve with a garnish of lamb's lettuce and lemon slices.

## SERVES 4

## PREPARATION TIME 10 MINUTES

## COOKING TIME 20 MINUTES

## INGREDIENTS

2 tbsp olive oil
2 red peppers, seeded and diced
½ leek, halved and sliced
2 cloves of garlic, minced
2 cooked chicken breasts, diced
350 g / 12 oz / 3 cups cooked short-grain rice
400 ml / 14 fl. oz / 1 ⅔ cups vegetable stock, hot
a pinch of saffron threads, infused in the stock
55 g / 2 oz / ½ cup Parmesan, finely grated
55 g / 2 oz / 1 cup lamb's lettuce
1 lemon, sliced
salt and freshly ground black pepper

**TOP TIP**

Remove the saffron threads before adding the stock.

# Quick Prep,
# Slow Cook

## QUICK PREP, SLOW COOK

# Almond Chicken Ragout

**SERVES 4**

**PREPARATION TIME 10 MINUTES**

**COOKING TIME 1 HOUR**

## INGREDIENTS

4 chicken thighs
4 chicken drumsticks
55 ml / 2 fl. oz / ¼ cup olive oil
1 onion, chopped
2 cloves of garlic, minced
2 tsp ground cumin
1 tsp ground coriander
½ tsp ground turmeric
100 g / 3 ½ oz / ⅔ cup raisins
1 tbsp honey
500 ml / 18 fl. oz / 2 cups chicken stock
2 tbsp flaked (slivered) almonds
salt and freshly ground black pepper

## METHOD

- Preheat the oven to 180°C (160°C fan) / 350F / gas 4.

- Coat the chicken pieces in the oil and season with salt and pepper. Heat a casserole dish over a moderate heat until hot. Seal the chicken in the oil until browned all over.

- Stir in the onion, garlic and a pinch of salt, frying for 2 minutes. Add the ground spices, raisins, honey and stock.

- Cover with a lid and transfer to the oven to bake for 45 minutes until the chicken is cooked through.

- Remove from the oven and adjust the seasoning to taste before serving scattered with almonds.

**TOP TIP**
Stir 2 tbsp of plain yoghurt into the gravy just before serving.

# Chicken Pie

**SERVES 4**

**PREPARATION TIME 15 MINUTES**

**COOKING TIME 45 MINUTES**

## INGREDIENTS

- tbsp butter, softened
- tbsp olive oil
- onions, chopped
- fennel bulbs, sliced
- skinless, boneless chicken thighs, diced
- 250 ml / 9 fl. oz / 1 cup chicken stock
- small bunch of thyme, leaves stripped
- 150 g / 5 oz ready-made puff pastry
- little plain (all-purpose) flour, for dusting
- salt and freshly ground black pepper

## METHOD

- Preheat the oven to 180°C (160°C fan) / 350F / gas 4. Grease a 900 g / 2 lb pudding bowl with the butter.

- Heat the oil in a large saucepan set over a medium heat until hot. Add the onion, fennel and a pinch of salt, sweating for 5 minutes until softened.

- Stir in the chicken and stock, cooking until simmering. Stir in the thyme and season to taste with salt and pepper.

- Spoon into the pudding bowl and lift the pudding bowl onto a baking tray. Roll out the pastry on a lightly floured surface into a round approximately to ½ cm (¼ in) thickness. Drape the pastry over the bowl and seal against the rim, cutting away the excess.

- Make a couple of slits in the top of the pastry and bake for 25–30 minutes until the pastry is golden and puffed.

- Remove to a wire rack before serving.

**TOP TIP**

For a glaze on the pastry, brush the top of it with a beaten egg yolk before baking.

# Glazed Chicken

**SERVES 4**

**PREPARATION TIME 10 MINUTES**

**COOKING TIME 1 HOUR**

## INGREDIENTS

4 chicken drumsticks, trimmed
4 shallots, halved
450 g / 1 lb / 3 cups new potatoes, halved
75 ml / 3 fl. oz / ⅓ cup olive oil
150 g / 5 oz / ⅔ cup sweet chilli (chili) sauce
1 tbsp white sesame seeds
salt and freshly ground black pepper

## METHOD

- Preheat the oven to 190°C (170°C fan) / 375F / gas 5.
- Toss the chicken, shallots and potatoes with the olive oil and seasoning in a large roasting tray.
- Cover the tray with a sheet of kitchen foil and roast in the oven for 30 minutes. Remove the foil after 30 minutes and spoon over the chilli sauce, stirring well.
- Roast for a further 20–25 minutes until glazed before serving with a garnish of sesame seeds.

**TOP TIP**

This recipe works equally well with chicken thighs.

# Beef Casserole

**SERVES 4**

**PREPARATION TIME 10 MINUTES**

**COOKING TIME 2 HOURS 20 MINUTES**

## INGREDIENTS

55 g / 2 oz / ⅓ cup plain (all-purpose) flour

1 kg / 2 lb 4 oz / 6 ⅔ cups stewing steak, trimmed and cubed

55 ml / 2 fl. oz / ¼ cup sunflower oil

150 g / 5 oz / 1 cup pancetta lardons

6 shallots, halved

4 large carrots, peeled and diced

225 g / 8 oz / 3 cups closed-cup mushrooms, brushed clean

250 ml / 9 fl. oz / 1 cup good-quality ale

750 ml / 1 pint 6 fl. oz / 3 cups beef stock

2 bay leaves

salt and freshly ground black pepper

## METHOD

- Preheat the oven to 160°C (140°C fan) / 300F / gas 2.

- Dust the steak with the flour and season with plenty of salt and pepper. Heat some of the oil in a large casserole dish set over a moderate heat until hot.

- Seal the beef in batches, using fresh oil for each batch. Once sealed, pour away all but 1 tbsp of the oil.

- Add the pancetta, shallots, carrots, mushrooms, ale, stock and bay leaves and bring to a simmer. Stir well and cover with a lid.

- Cook in the oven for 2 hours, stirring after 1 hour, until the beef is tender. Remove from the oven and adjust the seasoning to taste before serving.

**TOP TIP**

Red wine or stout can be used in place of the ale if preferred.

# Chilli con Carne

## METHOD

- Heat the oil in a large saucepan set over a medium heat until hot. Add the garlic and fry for 1 minute, stirring frequently.

- Add the beef mince and brown well all over, breaking it up with a wooden spoon. Stir in the ground spices and cook for a further minute.

- Cover with the passata, stock and beans. Stir well, cover with a lid and cook on a low heat for 1 hour.

- Once the chilli is ready, adjust the seasoning to taste. Serve with the rice and a garnish of red pepper and coriander.

## SERVES 4

## PREPARATION TIME 10 MINUTES

## COOKING TIME 1 HOUR 15 MINUTES

## INGREDIENTS

2 tbsp sunflower oil

2 cloves of garlic, minced

600 g / 1 lb 5 oz / 4 cups beef mince

2 tsp ground cumin

2 tsp ground coriander

2 tsp paprika

½ tsp chilli (chili) powder

400 ml / 14 fl. oz / 1 ⅔ cups passata

250 ml / 9 fl. oz / 1 cup beef stock, hot

400 g / 14 oz / 2 cups canned kidney beans, drained

350 g / 12 oz / 3 cups cooked long-grain rice, to serve

1 red pepper, seeded and sliced

a few sprigs of coriander (cilantro), to garnish

salt and freshly ground black pepper

**TOP TIP**

Give the chilli con carne a stir after 30 minutes of cooking.

# Lamb Rogan Josh

## METHOD

- Blend the onions, garlic, ginger and chillies with 55 ml / 2 fl. oz / ¼ cup of warm water in a food processor or blender.

- Heat the oil in a casserole dish set over a moderate heat until hot. Add the onion paste and fry for 3 minutes until it starts to brown.

- Add the ground spices, stir well and cook for a further minute. Stir in the lamb, passata and lamb stock.

- Cover with a lid and cook over a low heat for 1 hour. Remove the lid, stir well and cook for a further hour until the lamb is tender and the sauce has thickened.

- Adjust the seasoning to taste and serve with basmati rice.

**SERVES 4**

**PREPARATION TIME 10 MINUTES**

**COOKING TIME 2 HOURS 10 MINUTES**

## INGREDIENTS

2 onions, chopped
4 cloves of garlic, crushed
5 cm (2 in) piece of root ginger, peeled
2 red chillies (chilies), chopped
55 ml / 2 fl. oz / ¼ cup vegetable oil
2 tsp paprika
1 ½ tsp ground cumin
1 tsp ground coriander
1 tsp ground cardamom
¼ tsp ground cloves
750 g / 1 lb 10 oz / 5 cups lamb shoulder, diced
250 ml / 9 fl. oz / 1 cup passata
500 ml / 18 fl. oz / 2 cups lamb stock
450 g / 1 lb / 4 cups cooked basmati rice
salt and freshly ground black pepper

**TOP TIP**
Try stirring 2 tbsp of cream into the sauce for a cooling addition.

# Lamb and Olive Tagine

## SERVES 4

## PREPARATION TIME 10 MINUTES

## COOKING TIME 2 HOURS

## INGREDIENTS

55 ml / 2 fl. oz / ¼ cup olive oil
750 g / 1 lb 10 oz / 5 cups lamb neck fillet, diced
1 onion, chopped
2 cloves of garlic, chopped
1 red pepper, seeded and diced
1 green pepper, seeded and diced
4 Portobello mushrooms, peeled and diced
1 tbsp ras el hanout
2 tbsp honey
1 tbsp tomato purée
750 ml / 1 pint 6 fl. oz / 3 cups vegetable stock, hot
75 g / 3 oz / ½ cup pitted olives
salt and freshly ground black pepper

## METHOD

- Heat the olive oil in a tagine or casserole dish set over a moderate heat until hot.

- Add the lamb with seasoning and brown well all over. Stir in the onion, garlic, peppers, mushrooms and ground spices.

- Stir in the honey, tomato purée and stock. Cover with a lid and cook over a low heat for 1 hour 45–55 minutes until the lamb is tender.

- Stir in the olives and adjust the seasoning to taste before serving.

**TOP TIP**
Boneless lamb shoulder or leg can be used if neck fillet is not available.

# Cider, Pork and Bacon Pie

**ERVES 4**

**REPARATION TIME 15 MINUTES**

**OOKING TIME 50 MINUTES**

## INGREDIENTS

tbsp butter
25 g / 8 oz / 1 ½ cups bacon joint, diced
00 g / 1 lb 2 oz / 3 ⅓ cups pork loin, diced
Golden Delicious apple, cored and sliced
tbsp wholegrain mustard
00 ml / 18 fl. oz / 2 cups cider
00 g / 7 oz ready-made puff pastry
little plain (all-purpose) flour, for dusting
large egg, beaten
alt and freshly ground black pepper

## METHOD

- Preheat the oven to 180°C (160°C fan) / 350F / gas 4.

- Melt the butter in a large cast-iron frying pan set over a medium heat until hot. Add the bacon and fry for 3 minutes until golden.

- Add the pork and apple, stirring well. Cook for a further 3 minutes and then stir in the mustard and cider. Simmer for 5 minutes and adjust the seasoning to taste, setting the pan to one side.

- Roll out the pastry on a lightly floured surface into a round approximately 5 cm (2 in) wider than the diameter of the frying pan. The pastry should be approximately ½ cm (¼ in) thick.

- Cut the pastry to size and drape over the filling in the pan, tucking in the edges. Brush the top with the beaten egg and make three small slits in the top.

- Bake for 30–35 minutes until the pastry is golden and puffed before serving.

**TOP TIP**
Substitute the cider for half apple juice and half ham stock for a non-alcoholic version.

# Sticky Pork Ribs

## METHOD

- Preheat the oven to 160°C (140°C fan) / 300F / gas 2.

- Combine the sugar, paprika, garlic powder and seasoning in a bowl. Rub over the ribs on both sides.

- Sit the ribs on a baking tray lined with greaseproof paper. Cover the tray with a double-layer of aluminium foil, sealing it well.

- Bake for 2–2 ½ hours or until the meat starts to come away from the bone.

- Whisk together the barbecue sauce, tomato purée and lemon juice in a small bowl. Brush the pork ribs with the sauce on both sides.

- Preheat the grill to hot. Grill the ribs for 2 minutes on both sides, until bubbling and brown at the edges.

- Leave to sit briefly before serving.

## SERVES 4

## PREPARATION TIME 10 MINUTES

## COOKING TIME 2 HOURS 45 MINUTES

## INGREDIENTS

125 g / 4 ½ oz / ⅔ cup soft light brown sugar
1 tbsp paprika
1 tsp garlic powder
1.5 kg / 3 lb 5 oz rack of pork ribs, trimmed
225 g / 8 oz / 1 cup barbecue sauce
2 tbsp tomato purée
1 lemon, juiced
salt and freshly ground black pepper

**TOP TIP**
Add 1 tsp of Cayenne to the sugar and spice rub for spicy ribs.

QUICK PREP, SLOW COOK

# Sausage Cassoulet

**SERVES 4**

**PREPARATION TIME 10 MINUTES**

**COOKING TIME 1 HOUR**

## INGREDIENTS

tbsp olive oil
pork sausages
carrots, cut into sticks
red onions, cut into wedges
cloves of garlic, finely chopped
tbsp tomato purée
250 ml / 9 fl. oz / 1 cup red wine
750 ml / 1 pint 6 fl. oz / 3 cups beef stock
250 g / 9 oz / 1 ⅔ cups cherry tomatoes,
    halved
400 g / 14 oz / 2 cups canned white
    beans, drained
few sprigs of rosemary, chopped
salt and freshly ground black pepper

## METHOD

- Heat the oil in a large casserole dish set over a moderate heat until hot. Add the sausages and brown all over. Remove from the dish.

- Reduce the heat slightly and add the carrots, onions and garlic, cooking for 3 minutes. Stir in the tomato purée and then the red wine and stock.

- Stir in the cherry tomatoes, beans, rosemary and seasoning and cook at a simmer for 40–45 minutes until the vegetables and beans are tender.

- Return the sausages to the dish and heat through. Season to taste before serving.

**TOP TIP**
Prick the sausages with a fork before frying to prevent them popping or spitting.

QUICK PREP, SLOW COOK

# Fish Pie

## METHOD

- Preheat the oven to 180°C (160°C fan) / 350F / gas 4. Cook the potato in a large saucepan of salted boiling water for 15–18 minutes until tender to the point of a knife.

- Meanwhile, melt 2 tbsp of butter in a large saucepan set over a medium heat until hot. Add the leek and a pinch of salt, sweating for 5 minutes until soft.

- Remove the leek from the pan and melt a couple more tablespoons of butter. Whisk in the flour to make a roux, cooking it until golden in appearance. Whisk in the milk in a slow, steady stream until thickened.

- Simmer for 2 minutes and then stir in the fish and leek. Season with salt and pepper before spooning into a ceramic, oval baking dish.

- Drain the potato when ready and mash with the remaining butter, crème fraiche and seasoning. Spread over the filling in the dish using a fork.

- Bake for 40–45 minutes until golden on top. Leave to stand for 5 minutes before serving.

**SERVES 4**

**PREPARATION TIME 10 MINUTES**

**COOKING TIME 1 HOUR 10 MINUTES**

## INGREDIENTS

900 g / 2 lb / 6 cups floury potatoes, peeled and diced

75 g / 3 oz / ⅓ cup butter, cubed

1 leek, halved and sliced

2 tbsp plain (all-purpose) flour

600 ml / 1 pint 2 fl. oz / 2 ½ cups whole milk

300 g / 10 ½ oz / 2 cups skinless salmon fillet, diced

300 g / 10 ½ oz / 2 cups skinless cod fillet, diced

110 g / 4 oz / ½ cup crème fraiche

salt and freshly ground black pepper

**TOP TIP**

Wash the sliced leek in a bowl of cold water if it is particularly dirty or gritty.

# Spicy Prawn and Squash Curry

SERVES 4

PREPARATION TIME 10 MINUTES

COOKING TIME 1 HOUR

## INGREDIENTS

- 2 tbsp sunflower oil
- 2 tbsp Thai green curry paste
- ½ tsp chilli (chili) powder
- 1 small butternut squash, peeled and diced
- 400 ml / 14 fl. oz / 1 ⅔ cups coconut milk
- 500 ml / 18 fl. oz / 2 cups vegetable stock
- 450 g / 1 lb / 3 cups king prawns (shrimps), peeled and deveined
- 2 jalapeño peppers, sliced
- a small handful of coriander (cilantro), torn
- 1 lime, sliced
- 450 g / 1 lb / 4 cups cooked basmati rice
- salt and freshly ground black pepper

## METHOD

- Heat the oil in a saucepan set over a moderate heat until hot. Add the curry paste and chilli powder, frying for 1 minute, stirring continuously.

- Add the squash, stir well and cover with the coconut milk and stock. Cook at a gentle simmer for 40–45 minutes until tender.

- Add the prawns, stir well and continue to cook for a further 10 minutes over a reduced heat until they are pink and tender.

- Season to taste with salt and pepper. Serve the curry in bowls, garnished with the sliced jalapeño, coriander, lime slices and basmati rice.

**TOP TIP**

Give the curry a stir from time to time as it simmers.

# Meat-free Moussaka

## SERVES 4

## PREPARATION TIME 10 MINUTES

## COOKING TIME 1 HOUR 45 MINUTES

## INGREDIENTS

55 ml / 2 fl. oz / ¼ cup vegetable oil

2 large onions, chopped

2 cloves of garlic, minced

450 g / 16 oz / 3 cups vegetarian mince

2 tsp dried oregano

½ tsp ground cinnamon

400 g / 14 oz / 2 cups canned
    chopped tomatoes

225 ml / 8 fl. oz / 1 cup vegetable stock

75 g / 3 oz / ⅓ cup unsalted butter

75 g / 3 oz / ½ cup plain (all-purpose) flour

750 ml / 1 pint 6 fl. oz / 3 cups whole milk

2 small egg yolks

110 g / 4 oz / 1 cup Cheddar, grated

3 aubergines (eggplants), finely diced

55 g / 2 oz / ½ cup mozzarella, grated

salt and freshly ground black pepper

## METHOD

- Heat the oil in a large casserole dish set over a medium heat and sauté the onion and garlic for 5 minutes.

- Add the vegetarian mince and brown all over before stirring in the dried herbs and spices. Add the chopped tomatoes and vegetable stock. Simmer over a slightly reduced heat for 30 minutes.

- Preheat the oven to 180°C (160°C fan) / 350F / gas 4. Melt the butter in a large saucepan set over a moderate heat and whisk in the flour to make a roux, cooking until golden.

- Whisk in the milk in a slow, steady stream until thickened. Simmer for 5 minutes, then whisk in the egg yolks, half the Cheddar and some seasoning.

- Layer the sauce, aubergine and cheese sauce in a large oval baking dish. Finish with a layer of cheese sauce on top followed with the remaining grated Cheddar and mozzarella on top.

- Bake for 50–60 minutes until golden and bubbling on top.

**TOP TIP**

Top the moussaka with a layer of soft goats' cheese for a tangy addition.

# Vegetable Lasagne

**SERVES 4**

**PREPARATION TIME 10 MINUTES**

**COOKING TIME 1 HOUR 20 MINUTES**

## INGREDIENTS

- 75 ml / 2 fl. oz / ¼ cup olive oil
- 2 onions, chopped
- 2 sticks of celery, chopped
- 2 cloves of garlic, minced
- 1 leek, halved and sliced
- 2 courgettes (zucchinis), sliced
- 400 g / 14 oz / 2 cups canned chopped tomatoes
- 400 ml / 14 fl. oz / 1 ¾ cups passata
- 1 pinch of dried oregano
- 450 g / 1 lb / 4 cups lasagne sheets
- 300 g / 10 ½ oz / 1 ½ cups ricotta
- 100 g / 3 ½ oz / 1 cup mozzarella, grated
- 1 small handful of basil leaves
- Salt and freshly ground black pepper

## METHOD

- Heat the olive oil in a casserole dish set over a medium heat until hot. Add the onion, celery, garlic, leek, courgette and a pinch of salt, sweating for 10 minutes until softened.

- Add the chopped tomatoes, passata and oregano. Stir well and simmer briefly, seasoning with salt and pepper.

- Preheat the oven to 180°C (160°C fan) / 350F / gas 4 and line a large rectangular baking dish with some lasagne sheets.

- Top with some of the vegetable sauce and follow with some of the ricotta. Repeat the layering with lasagne sheets, vegetable sauce and ricotta.

- Finish with a layer of lasagne sheets and sprinkle over the mozzarella. Bake for 1 hour until golden.

- Leave the lasagne to stand for 5 minutes and garnish with basil leaves before serving.

**TOP TIP**
Grease the baking dish with a little olive oil before layering the lasagne.

# Lentil Stew

## METHOD

- Heat the oil in a casserole dish set over a medium heat until hot. Add the onion, garlic, peppers and a pinch of salt.
- Sweat for 5 minutes, stirring occasionally. Add the lentils, chopped tomatoes, beans and stock, stirring well.
- Cover with a lid and cook at a gentle simmer for 50–60 minutes until the lentils are tender.
- Add the broad beans, asparagus and baby spinach, stirring well. Cover with a lid and cook for a further 5 minutes.
- Season to taste with salt and pepper. Ladle into bowls and serve with a garnish of basil leaves.

## SERVES 4

## PREPARATION TIME 10 MINUTES

## COOKING TIME 1 HOUR 15 MINUTES

## INGREDIENTS

2 tbsp olive oil
1 onion, finely chopped
2 cloves of garlic, minced
1 red pepper, seeded and chopped
1 yellow pepper, seeded and chopped
175 g / 6 oz / 1 cup red lentils
400 g / 14 oz / 2 cups canned
    chopped tomatoes
400 g / 14 oz / 2 cups canned black eyed
    beans, drained
1 l / 1 pint 16 fl. oz / 4 cups vegetable stock
150 g / 5 oz / 1 ½ cups broad (fava)
    beans, shelled
150 g / 5 oz / 1 ½ cups asparagus spears,
    woody ends removed and halved
100 g / 3 ½ oz / 2 cups baby spinach, washed
a small handful of basil leaves
salt and freshly ground black pepper

**TOP TIP**
Make a little extra stock so you can top it up if the stew starts to run dry.

# Stuffed Mushrooms

SERVES 4

PREPARATION TIME 15 MINUTES

COOKING TIME 40 MINUTES

## INGREDIENTS

300 g / 10 ½ oz / 4 cups closed-cup mushrooms, brushed clean with stems removed

1 large head of broccoli, diced

1 red pepper, seeded and finely diced

1 shallot, finely chopped

2 cloves of garlic, minced

55 g / 2 oz / 1 cup fresh breadcrumbs

150 g / 5 oz / 1 ½ cups Parmesan, grated

55 ml / 2 fl. oz / ¼ cup olive oil

½ tsp paprika

salt and freshly ground black pepper

## METHOD

- Preheat the oven to 180°C (160°C fan) / 350F / gas 4. Arrange the mushrooms, cap-side down, in a large roasting dish lined with aluminium foil.

- Toss together the broccoli, pepper, shallot, garlic, breadcrumbs and 100 g / 3 ½ oz / 1 cup of the Parmesan. Season with salt and pepper.

- Pack the mixture onto the mushrooms and drizzle with olive oil.

- Cover the roasting dish with a sheet of kitchen foil and bake for 25 minutes.

- Remove the foil after 25 minutes and continue baking for a further 10–15 minutes until the mushrooms are crisp on top.

- Remove from the oven and garnish with the remaining Parmesan and a pinch of paprika.

**TOP TIP**

If the mushrooms are dirty, wash them in a bowl of cold water.

# Winter Vegetable Stew

**SERVES 4**

**PREPARATION TIME 10 MINUTES**

**COOKING TIME 1 HOUR 15 MINUTES**

## INGREDIENTS

2 tbsp olive oil

1 onion, chopped

2 cloves of garlic, chopped

450 g / 1 lb / 3 cups carrots, chopped

2 sticks of celery, chopped

400 g / 14 oz / 2 cups canned white
    beans, drained

300 g / 10 ½ oz / 2 cups ripe tomatoes, quartered

200 g / 7 oz / 1 cup passata

1 l / 1 pint 16 fl. oz / 4 cups vegetable stock

250 g / 9 oz / 2 cups cavolo nero, chopped

100 g / 3 ½ oz / ½ cup basil pesto, to serve

salt and freshly ground black pepper

## METHOD

- Heat the oil in a large casserole dish set over a medium heat until hot.

- Add the onion, carrots, celery and a pinch of salt, sweating for 5 minutes until softened.

- Add the remaining ingredients apart from the cavolo nero and basil pesto. Stir well, cover with a lid and cook over a low heat for 1 hour until the beans are tender.

- Stir in the cavolo nero and cook for a further 10 minutes. Season to taste with salt and pepper.

- Ladle into bowls and serve with the basil pesto on the side.

**TOP TIP**

Serve this soup with a fresh grating of Parmesan on top.

# Simple Desserts and Snacks

# Apple and Blackberry Crumble

**SERVES 4**

**PREPARATION TIME 10 MINUTES**

**COOKING TIME 20 MINUTES**

## INGREDIENTS

2 large Bramley apples, peeled and diced
450 g / 1 lb / 3 cups blackberries
1 tbsp lemon juice
2 tbsp caster (superfine) sugar
175 g / 6 oz / 1 ¼ cups plain (all-purpose)
    flour
150 g / 5 oz / ⅔ cup unsalted butter, cubed
125 g / 4 ½ oz / ⅔ cup soft light brown sugar
½ tsp ground cinnamon
a pinch of salt

## METHOD

- Preheat the oven to 200°C (180°C fan) / 400F / gas 6.
- Combine the apple, blackberries, lemon juice, caster sugar and 2 tbsp of water in a large saucepan.
- Cover and cook over a medium heat until the apple starts to soften and break down.
- Meanwhile, pulse together the flour, butter, brown sugar, cinnamon and salt in a food processor until it resembles breadcrumbs.
- Spread out the mixture on a large baking tray. Bake for 8–10 minutes until golden and toasted.
- Spoon the fruit mixture onto serving plates and top with the crumble before serving.

**TOP TIP**

For a different texture, add a handful of oats to the crumble mixture before baking.

# Baked Chocolate Mousse

**SERVES 4**

**PREPARATION TIME 15 MINUTES**

**COOKING TIME 25 MINUTES**

## INGREDIENTS

110 ml / 4 fl. oz / ½ cup water

55 g / 2 oz / ⅓ cup cocoa powder

1 tbsp brandy

150 g / 5 oz / 1 cup dark chocolate, grated

2 large eggs

2 large egg whites

75 g / 3 oz / ⅓ cup caster (superfine) sugar

a pinch of salt

## METHOD

- Preheat the oven to 200°C (180°C fan) / 400F / gas 6.

- Place the water in a saucepan and heat until boiling. Whisk in the cocoa powder and brandy until smooth.

- Gently whisk in the chocolate, off the heat, until smooth. Leave to cool for 5 minutes.

- Combine the eggs, egg whites, sugar and salt in a heatproof bowl set over a saucepan of half-filled simmering water.

- Cook the mixture, whisking constantly, until it registers 115°C / 239F on a sugar thermometer. Remove the bowl from the heat and continue to beat for 4–5 minutes until the mixture leaves a ribbon-like trail.

- Stir one third of the egg mixture into the chocolate mixture. Fold the chocolate mixture into the remaining egg mixture with a rubber spatula.

- Divide the mixture between four individual heatproof glasses and place on a baking tray. Bake for 15 minutes until set.

**TOP TIP**

Swap the brandy for 1 tsp of orange flower water for a non-alcoholic version.

# Tiramisu

## METHOD

- Whip together the cream, mascarpone, sugar and 1 tbsp of Marsala until softly peaked and floppy.
- Soak the sponge fingers in a mixture of coffee and the remaining Marsala. Position two-thirds of the soaked fingers in the base of four serving glasses.
- Top with some of the whipped cream mixture and then top with the remaining soaked sponge fingers.
- Spoon over the remaining cream mixture and grate dark chocolate on top before serving.

## SERVES 4

## PREPARATION TIME 15 MINUTES

## INGREDIENTS

250 ml / 9 fl. oz / 1 cup whipping cream, cold
250 g / 9 oz / 1 cup mascarpone
75 g / 3 oz / ⅓ cup caster (superfine) sugar
110 ml / 4 fl. oz / ½ cup Marsala
16 savoiardi sponge fingers, chopped
225 ml / 8 fl. oz / 1 cup brewed coffee, cold
55 g / 2 oz / ⅓ cup dark chocolate

**TOP TIP**

These deserts can be made ahead of time and chilled until ready to serve.

# Sticky Toffee Puds

SERVES 4

PREPARATION TIME 15 MINUTES

COOKING TIME 45 MINUTES

## INGREDIENTS

225 g / 8 oz / 1 cup unsalted butter, softened

200 g / 7 oz / 1 ¼ cups pitted dates

110 ml / 4 fl. oz / ½ cup water

1 tsp baking powder

300 g / 10 ½ oz / 1 ¾ cups soft brown sugar

2 large eggs

1 tsp vanilla extract

½ tsp bicarbonate of (baking) soda

225 g / 8 oz / 1 ½ cups plain (all-purpose) flour, sifted

150 ml / 5 fl. oz / ⅔ cup double (heavy) cream

2 tbsp golden syrup

## METHOD

- Preheat the oven to 180°C (160°C fan) / 350F / gas 4. Grease four individual ramekins with a little of the butter.

- Combine the dates, water and bicarbonate of soda in a saucepan, warming over a medium heat until it approaches boiling point. Remove from the heat and set to one side.

- Cream together 175 g / 6 oz / 1 cup of the sugar with 110 g / 4 oz / ½ cup of the butter in a separate bowl until pale.

- Beat in the eggs, one by one and then beat in the vanilla extract and baking powder. Fold through the flour in thirds and then the date mixture.

- Spoon into the ramekins and bake for 30–35 minutes until risen and a cake tester comes out almost clean from their centres. Remove the puddings from the oven and leave to cool slightly on a wire rack.

- Warm together the cream and golden syrup with the remaining sugar and butter in a saucepan set over a medium heat, stirring, until smooth and thickened.

- Turn out the puddings and serve with the sauce.

**TOP TIP**

Add 2 tbsp of dark rum to the sauce for a boozy version.

# Tarte Tatin

## METHOD

- Heat together the butter and sugar in an ovenproof frying pan or tatin dish until melted, stirring occasionally.

- Remove the pan from the heat and arrange the apples in the pan, cut-side up, fitting them together neatly. Return the pan to a reduced heat.

- Cook for 10 minutes. Preheat the oven to 220°C (200°C fan) / 425F / gas 7.

- Roll out the pastry on a lightly floured surface into a round approximately 5 cm (2 in) wider than the diameter of the frying pan. The pastry should be approximately 1 cm (½ in) thick.

- Drape the pastry over the apples, tucking the edges in between the apples and the side of the pan.

- Bake for 20 minutes until the pastry is golden and puffed. Remove from the oven and run the tip of a knife around the inside of the pan to loosen. Carefully invert onto a plate before serving.

## SERVES 4

## PREPARATION TIME 15 MINUTES

## COOKING TIME 35 MINUTES

## INGREDIENTS

150 g / 5 oz / ⅔ cup unsalted butter, cubed

225 g / 8 oz / 1 cup caster (superfine) sugar

7 small Golden Delicious apples, peeled, cored and halved

225 g / 8 oz ready-made puff pastry

a little plain (all-purpose) flour, for dusting

**TOP TIP**

This dessert should be served with vanilla ice cream or crème fraiche on the side.

# Eton Mess

## METHOD

- Purée half the strawberries with 2 tbsp of icing sugar and the lemon juice in a food processor or blender.

- Pass the purée through a fine sieve and set to one side.

- Whip the cream in a mixing bowl with the remaining sugar and vanilla extract until softly peaked.

- Fill four serving glasses with the crumbled meringue, whipped cream and remaining strawberries.

- Drizzle over the strawberry sauce before serving.

## SERVES 4

## PREPARATION TIME 10 MINUTES

## INGREDIENTS

450 g / 1 lb / 3 cups strawberries, hulled and halved

55 g / 2 ½ oz / ½ cup icing (confectioners') sugar, sifted

½ lemon, juiced

250 ml / 9 fl. oz / 1 cup whipping cream

½ tsp vanilla extract

4 large meringue nests, crumbled

**TOP TIP**
This dessert can be made with raspberries or blueberries as well.

# Blackcurrant Trifle

## SERVES 4

## PREPARATION TIME 10 MINUTES

## COOKING TIME 15 MINUTES

## INGREDIENTS

1 orange
450 g / 1 lb / 4 cups blackcurrants
65 g / 2 ½ oz / ½ cup icing (confectioners')
    sugar
250 ml / 9 fl. oz / 1 cup double (heavy) cream
½ tsp vanilla extract
450 g / 16 oz piece of sponge cake, cubed

## METHOD

- Pare the zest from the orange and julienne. Juice the orange into a saucepan and add the blackcurrants and the icing sugar.

- Cover with a lid and cook over a low heat, stirring occasionally, until the blackcurrants are soft and juicy. Remove from the heat and leave to cool.

- Whip together the cream and vanilla extract in a mixing bowl until softly peaked.

- Spoon half of the cream into four serving glasses and top with the cooled blackcurrants and some of the juice.

- Top with some cubed sponge and more blackcurrants. Repeat with another layer of cream, blackcurrants and sponge.

- Finish with a final layer of blackcurrants. Garnish with orange zest before serving.

**TOP TIP**
This recipe works really well with the same amount of blueberries.

# Orange Custard Tarts

**MAKES 4**

**PREPARATION TIME 15 MINUTES**

**COOKING TIME 15 MINUTES**

## INGREDIENTS

2 oranges

225 g / 8 oz / 1 cup caster (superfine) sugar

1 tbsp cornflour (cornstarch)

150 ml / 5 fl oz / ⅔ cup fresh orange juice

150 ml / 5 fl oz / ⅔ cup water

175 g / 6 oz / ¾ cup unsalted butter, cubed

4 medium egg yolks

3 medium eggs

4 ready-made pastry tartlet cases

1 tbsp icing (confectioners') sugar

## METHOD

- Pare the zest from one orange and julienne. Segment both oranges into a bowl, cover and chill until needed.

- Combine the caster sugar, cornflour, orange juice and water in a saucepan. Cook over a low heat until bubbling.

- Remove from the heat and beat in the butter, one cube at a time, until incorporated. Beat in the egg yolks and eggs.

- Cook over a low heat, stirring, for a few minutes until the custard has thickened.

- Fill the tartlet cases with the custard and top with icing sugar, orange segments and julienned zest. Glaze the tops of the tarts with a chef's blowtorch before serving.

**TOP TIP**

Garnish and glaze with a blowtorch just before serving.

# Rice Pudding with Chocolate

**SERVES 4**

**PREPARATION TIME 5 MINUTES**

**COOKING TIME 15 MINUTES**

## INGREDIENTS

2 tbsp unsalted butter

450 g / 1 lb / 4 cups cooked short-grain rice

75 g / 3 oz / ⅓ cup golden caster
   (superfine) sugar

350 ml / 12 fl. oz / 1 ½ cups semi-skimmed
   milk

350 ml / 12 fl. oz / 1 ½ cups evaporated milk

½ tsp vanilla extract

100 g / 3 ½ oz / ⅔ cup dark chocolate, chopped

## METHOD

- Melt the butter in a large saucepan
  set over a medium heat until hot.

- Add the rice and sugar, stirring well.
  Cover with the milk, evaporated
  milk and vanilla extract.

- Stir well, cover with a lid and cook
  for 5 minutes or until the sugar has
  dissolved and the pudding is creamy.
  Remove the lid and stir in a quarter
  of the chocolate.

- Continue to cook, over a low heat,
  for a further 5 minutes until the
  chocolate has been incorporated.

- Spoon into bowls and top with the
  remaining chocolate before serving.

**TOP TIP**

Try this pudding with
white chocolate and a
few raspberries
on top.

# Mini Meringues

**MAKES 8**

**PREPARATION TIME 20 MINUTES**

**COOKING TIME 40 MINUTES**

## INGREDIENTS

150 g / 5 oz / 1 cup redcurrants

65 g / 2 ½ oz / ½ cup icing (confectioners')
    sugar

1 tbsp lemon juice

4 medium egg whites

1 pinch of salt

½ tsp cream of tartar

225 g / 8 oz / 1 cup caster (superfine) sugar

## METHOD

- Preheat the oven to 150°C (130°C fan) / 300F / gas 2. Line two baking trays with greaseproof paper.

- Purée the redcurrants with the icing sugar and lemon juice in a food processor or blender until smooth. Pass through a fine sieve into a bowl.

- Beat the egg whites with a pinch of salt in a large, clean mixing bowl until stiffly peaked. Add the cream of tartar and then beat in half of the sugar. Beat in the remaining sugar until fully dissolved and the meringue is thick and glossy.

- Swirl half of the redcurrant purée into the meringue mixture. Spoon rounds onto the lined trays and top with more of the redcurrant purée.

- Bake for 40 minutes until firm and set.

**TOP TIP**

For a drier texture, bake these meringues at 140°C (120°C fan) / 275F / gas 1 for 1 hour.

# Easy Ice Cream

**SERVES 4**

**PREPARATION TIME 30 MINUTES**

## INGREDIENTS

300 ml / 10 ½ fl. oz / 1 ⅓ cups double
    (heavy) cream

300 ml / ½ pt / 1 ¼ cups sweetened condensed
    milk, cold

55 g / 2 oz / ⅓ cup cocoa powder

½ tsp vanilla extract

100 g / 3 ½ oz / ⅔ cup dark chocolate, chopped

chocolate sticks, to serve

## METHOD

- Whisk together the cream,
  condensed milk, cocoa powder
  and vanilla extract until the cocoa
  powder has dissolved.

- Pour the mixture into an ice cream
  machine and churn according to the
  manufacturer's instructions, adding
  the chocolate after 5 minutes, until
  soft yet frozen.

- Scoop into bowls and serve with the
  chocolate sticks on the side.

**TOP TIP**

For a firmer texture,
freeze the ice cream
after churning before
serving.

# Raspberry Sorbet

SERVES 4

PREPARATION TIME 30 MINUTES

COOKING TIME 5 MINUTES

## INGREDIENTS

250 ml / 9 fl. oz / 1 cup water
400 g / 14 oz / 2 ⅔ cups raspberries
100 g / 3 ½ oz / ½ cup caster (superfine) sugar

## METHOD

- Combine the water, raspberries and sugar in a saucepan and cook over a medium heat until softened.

- Blend the mixture in a food processor until smooth. Pass it through a sieve into the bowl of an ice cream machine.

- Churn the mixture according to the manufacturer's instructions until frozen and set.

- Serve the sorbet straight away or cover and leave it to freeze for 2 hours until firm.

**TOP TIP**
Warm an ice cream scoop in hot water before scooping out the sorbet.

# Chocolate Cupcakes

## METHOD

- Preheat the oven to 180°C (160°C fan) / 350F / gas 4 and line a 12-hole cupcake tin with cases.
- Beat together the flour, cocoa powder, margarine, sugar, eggs and milk in a large mixing bowl until smooth; this should take about 2 minutes.
- Spoon into the cases and bake for 18–22 minutes until risen and springy to the touch.
- Remove to a wire rack to cool.
- Briefly stir together the butter, icing sugar and hot water, then add the chocolate sauce and beat until smooth.
- Spoon into a piping bag fitted with a star-shaped nozzle. Pipe swirls of the buttercream on top of the cupcakes. Garnish with a sugar rose on top before serving.

## MAKES 12

## PREPARATION TIME 20 MINUTES

## COOKING TIME 25 MINUTES

## INGREDIENTS

110 g / 4 oz / ⅔ cup self-raising flour, sifted

2 tbsp cocoa powder

110 g / 4 oz / ½ cup margarine, softened

110 g / 4 oz / ½ cup golden caster (superfine) sugar

2 large eggs

2 tbsp whole milk

225 g / 8 oz / 1 cup butter, softened

125 g / 4 ½ oz / 1 cup icing (confectioners') sugar

2 tbsp hot water

55 g / 2 oz / ¼ cup chocolate sauce

12 sugar roses, to garnish

**TOP TIP**

After filling the cases with batter, tap the tin on a flat surface to settle the batter.

# Chocolate Brownies

**MAKES 12**

**PREPARATION TIME 10 MINUTES**

**COOKING TIME 50 MINUTES**

## INGREDIENTS

350 g / 12 oz / 2 ⅓ cups dark chocolate, chopped

225 g / 8 oz / 1 cup unsalted butter, softened

3 large eggs

250 g / 9 oz / 1 ⅓ cups soft light brown sugar

125 g / 4 ½ oz / ¾ cup plain (all-purpose) flour

½ tsp baking powder

a pinch of salt

110 g / 4 oz / 1 cup walnut halves, chopped

2 tbsp cocoa powder

milk, to serve

## METHOD

- Preheat the oven to 170°C (150°C fan) / 325F / gas 3. Grease and line and 20 cm (8 in) square baking tin with greaseproof paper.

- Melt together the chocolate and butter in a saucepan set over a medium heat, stirring occasionally until smooth. Remove from the heat and allow to cool a little.

- In a large mixing bowl, whisk the eggs until thick and then beat in the sugar until thick and glossy.

- Beat in the melted chocolate mixture and then fold in the flour, baking powder, salt and chopped walnuts.

- Pour into the baking tin and tap lightly a few times to release any trapped air bubbles.

- Bake for 35–40 minutes until the surface has set; test with a wooden toothpick, if it comes out almost clean, the brownie is done.

- Remove to a wire rack to cool. Dust with cocoa powder before turning out, slicing and serving with glasses of milk.

**TOP TIP**
Let the brownie cool completely before turning out and slicing.

# Lemon Curd Tartlets

**SERVES 4**

**PREPARATION TIME 20 MINUTES**

**COOKING TIME 30 MINUTES**

## INGREDIENTS

250 g / 9 oz ready-made shortcrust pastry
a little plain (all-purpose) flour, for dusting
225 g / 8 oz / 1 cup caster (superfine) sugar
2 tbsp cornflour (cornstarch)
250 ml / 9 fl. oz / 1 cup fresh lemon juice
150 ml / 5 fl. oz / ⅔ cup water
175 g / 6 oz / ¾ cup unsalted butter, cubed
6 medium egg yolks
2 medium eggs
2 tbsp icing (confectioners') sugar
1 lemon, cut into small triangles

## METHOD

- Preheat the oven to 180°C (160°C fan) / 350F / gas 4.

- Roll out the pastry on a floured surface to ½ cm (¼ in) thickness and cut into four rounds that will line the base and sides of four individual tartlet cases.

- Line the cases with the pastry and prick the base with a fork, cutting away any excess pastry. Line with cling film and fill with baking beans. Blind-bake for 15 minutes and then remove to a wire rack to cool.

- Mix the sugar, cornflour, lemon juice and water in a saucepan, cooking over a low heat until bubbling.

- Remove from the heat and beat in the butter, one cube at a time, until incorporated. Beat in the egg yolks and eggs, one by one.

- Cook over a low heat for a few minutes, stirring frequently, until the curd thickens and reaches dropping consistency.

- Fill the pastry cases with curd and garnish with the lemon triangles and a dusting of icing sugar.

**TOP TIP**

Dropping consistency is reached when a small amount of the curd drops off the spoon.

# Blueberry Muffins

**MAKES 18**

**PREPARATION TIME 10 MINUTES**

**COOKING TIME 25 MINUTES**

## INGREDIENTS

- non-fat cooking spray
- 450 g / 1 lb / 3 cups plain (all-purpose) flour, sifted
- 225 g / 8 oz / 1 cup caster (superfine) sugar
- 1 tsp baking powder
- 1 tsp bicarbonate of (baking) soda
- pinch of salt
- 75 g / 3 oz / ⅓ cup unsalted butter, melted and cooled
- 125 g / 4 ½ oz / ½ cup plain yoghurt
- 2 medium eggs
- 1 tsp vanilla extract
- 250 g / 9 oz / 2 cups blueberries
- 75 g / 2 oz / ¼ cup granulated sugar

## METHOD

- Preheat the oven to 180°C (160°C fan) / 350F / gas 4. Grease the insides of 18 cupcake or muffin cases with non-fat cooking spray.

- Combine the flour, sugar, baking powder, bicarbonate of soda and salt in a large mixing bowl.

- In a separate mixing bowl, whisk together the butter, yoghurt, eggs and vanilla extract until smooth.

- Add to the dry ingredients and fold through until just combined. Fold in the blueberries and divide the batter between the cases, topping with some granulated sugar.

- Arrange the cases on baking trays and bake for 22–25 minutes until risen, golden and springy to the touch; a toothpick will come out almost clean from their centres when they are ready.

- Remove to a wire rack to cool before turning out the muffins and serving.

**TOP TIP**

Avoid over-mixing the batter; it should be just combined rather than perfectly smooth.

# Rocky Road

**MAKES 24**

**PREPARATION TIME 10 MINUTES**

**COOKING TIME 10 MINUTES**

## INGREDIENTS

350 g / 12 oz / 2 ⅓ cups dark chocolate,
   chopped
55 g / 2 oz / ¼ cup unsalted butter
400 ml / 14 fl. oz / 1 ⅔ cups sweetened
   condensed milk
300 g / 10 ½ oz / 12 cups mini marshmallows
225 g / 8 oz / 1 ½ cups digestive biscuits,
   chopped
2 tbsp icing (confectioners') sugar

## METHOD

- Grease and line the base and sides of
  a 23 cm (9 in) square baking tin with
  greaseproof paper.

- Combine the chocolate and butter in
  a heatproof bowl set atop a half-filled
  saucepan of simmering water. Stir
  occasionally until melted.

- Remove the bowl from the heat and
  stir in the condensed milk until
  incorporated. Add the marshmallows
  and chopped biscuits, stirring well.

- Pour and scrape into the prepared
  tin. Leave to cool briefly and then
  cover and chill until set.

- Turn out and dust with icing sugar
  before cutting into squares.

**TOP TIP**
Add chopped glacé
cherries with the
marshmallows for a
fruity addition.

# Scones

MAKES 16

PREPARATION TIME 15 MINUTES

COOKING TIME 15 MINUTES

## INGREDIENTS

350 g / 12 oz / 2 ⅓ cups self-raising flour,
plus extra for dusting

1 tsp baking powder

a pinch of salt

100 g / 3 ½ oz / ½ cup butter, cubed

2 tbsp caster sugar

100 g / 3 ½ oz / ⅔ cup raisins

200 ml / 7 fl. oz / 1 cup semi-skimmed
milk, warmed

1 tsp vanilla extract

1 tbsp lemon juice

blackcurrant jam (jelly), to serve

clotted cream, to serve

## METHOD

- Preheat the oven to 200°C (180°C fan) / 400F / gas 6.

- Stir together the flour, baking powder and salt in a large mixing bowl. Add the butter and rub into the flour with your fingertips until it resembles rough breadcrumbs.

- Stir in the sugar and then add the raisins, warmed milk, vanilla extract and lemon juice, mixing until a dough comes together.

- Dust a work surface with flour and fold the dough on it a few times. Pat and shape into a round approximately 4 cm (1 ½ in) thick.

- Use a 5 cm (2 in) straight-sided cutter to stamp out rounds of the dough. Arrange on a large baking tray, spaced apart.

- Bake for 12–14 minutes until golden on top and risen. Remove to a wire rack to cool before serving with jam and clotted cream.

**TOP TIP**

Warm the milk in a microwave for 20–30 seconds to get the right temperature.

217

# Triple Choc Cookies

## MAKES 18

## PREPARATION TIME 15 MINUTES

## COOKING TIME 15 MINUTES

## INGREDIENTS

110 g / 4 oz / ½ cup unsalted butter, softened

175 g / 6 oz / ¾ cup caster (superfine) sugar

1 large egg

1 tsp vanilla extract

150 g / 5 oz / 1 cup plain (all-purpose) flour, sifted

55 g / 2 oz / ⅓ cup cocoa powder

½ tsp bicarbonate of (baking) soda

75 g / 3 oz / ½ cup milk chocolate chunks

75 g / 3 oz / ½ cup dark chocolate chunks

## METHOD

- Preheat the oven to 180°C (160°C fan) / 350F / gas 4 and line two large baking trays with greaseproof paper.

- Cream together the butter, sugar, egg and vanilla in a large mixing bowl until pale and fluffy.

- Fold in the flour, cocoa powder and bicarbonate of soda mixing well until a cookie dough comes together.

- Add the dark and milk chocolate chunks, folding them evenly into the batter.

- Drop tablespoons of the dough onto the baking trays, spaced apart.

- Bake for 12–15 minutes until set. Remove to a wire rack to cool before serving.

**TOP TIP**

For chewier cookies, remove them from the oven after 10 minutes and leave to cool.

# INDEX